The Caring Touch

JOHN W PRATT MA
Senior Lecturer in Psychology
Department of Health Studies
Sheffield City Polytechnic
Sheffield

ALLEN MASON BA MCSP DipTP
Senior Lecturer in Health Studies
Sheffield City Polytechnic
Sheffield

HM+M PUBLISHERS
London

© *J W Pratt   A Mason 1981*

HM+M **HM+M PUBLISHERS LTD** ARE A DIVISION OF
+M HEYDEN & SON LTD

England — Spectrum House, Hillview Gardens, London NW4 2JQ
Germany — Devesburgstrasse 6, 4440 Rheine
USA — 247 South 41st Street, Philadelphia PA 19104

ISBN 0 85602 093 1

Printed in Great Britain by
Mackays of Chatham Ltd

Contents

Preface

This book was originally conceived through the cross-fertilisation of two disciplines – psychology and physiotherapy.

John Pratt was trained as a schoolteacher specialising in physical education, later qualifying as an occupational psychologist with some commitment to the humanistic approaches, especially in the practices of the helping professions. Allen Mason is a physiotherapist and a lecturer in health studies, whose broader interests include alternative medicine and the philosophical and historical aspects of the healing process.

This combination of interests has led to an increasing concern about the 'academisation' of professional education and training and the urgent need to restore the balance a little, by giving some consideration to the art and practice of health care; particularly, it is felt necessary to examine the evidence for touching as an integral part of the healing process, both from the physical and from the psychological viewpoint.

This book, then, is intended to reach all those whose concern is for the healing of others. The term healing is used deliberately in a broad sense, to encompass both somatic and psychological elements, for we argue that these two are largely inseparable, and attempts to heal that focus on one or other part exclusively are less likely to succeed than an approach which looks at the 'whole person'.

While we are primarily interested in the attention of nurses, physiotherapists, occupational and other therapists and doctors, we are aware that the business of healing is not

confined to these people alone. Appreciation of the importance of touch in human relationships will be of use to those
whose work is not remedial in the strict sense of the word,
and in this category one might include the client himself,
teachers, parents, friends and ultimately our fellow humans
whoever and wherever they may be. Each of us has a role
to play whether it is in the emergency of sudden and public
collapse, or whether it is in the long-term responsibility for
children, family or friends.

There are two more groups whose interests are served; one
is the teachers of health professionals whose job it is to
educate and train the practitioner in the promotion and
maintenance of health and well-being. Although there has
been some shift of emphasis in basic courses to accommodate
the psychological aspect in healing, this is often undervalued
or unrecognised. A closer awareness of the effects of touching
in this context must constitute a significant part of such a
perspective. The other group is the academic and general
psychologists, sociologists and social workers who may not
fully appreciate what is already known of the nature and
effects of human touching, particularly in the contexts of
communication, development, normal function and well
being.

Our aim in writing this book is to encourage health professionals and others to be more aware of their practice in
making physical contact with others. It is hoped that some
knowledge of the health-promoting effects of contact will
foster a reappraisal and extension of present practices to the
ultimate benefit of client and healer. This aim may run
counter to trends in professional development where the
pursuit of status and increased autonomy has inevitably led
to greater emphasis being placed on academic learning rather
than on the application of practical and personal skills. To
some extent, therefore, it is a plea for careful consideration
of working with one's hands; a case against the mechanis-
ation and dehumanisation of the healing process; and a
demand for the re-establishment of modes of therapy that

make the best possible use of touch as a personal manifestation of caring.

Beyond this, we would wish to persuade people in general of the importance and value of being in physical contact with one another. Our society has fairly well defined and rather restrictive sanctions on its acts of touching. As a nation we have an international reputation for being reserved, and such public touching as occurs between adults is extremely limited. The significance of close bodily contact, especially in early childhood is discussed in chapter three and the inference here is that we may be depriving ourselves of essential developmental, social or therapeutic experience.

In order to achieve these aims and to support a prescriptive claim for the use of touch, we attempt to provide an academic and theoretical basis for tactile aspects of the client/healer interaction which have not yet been critically examined. The purpose and interpretation of touch in a clinical or any other situation, varies considerably according to the individual on either side of the transaction. Its effects, therefore, will vary, as will the well-being of the client. Chapter six tries to explain and to order these psychological effects and to establish their significance in the practice of therapy or medicine.

The practitioner/client relationship is a complex one, frequently depending on intuitive judgements from both parties. Becoming aware of self and of the use of touch in establishing and maintaining this relationship is one of several ways in which the practitioner comes to terms with the process of healing which as an art defies analysis and description.

This book both develops the theme of touch as a medium for healing and at the same time acknowledges that its effects are sometimes beyond scientific explanation, depending as it does on the unique characteristics of the people involved.

JOHN W. PRATT

ALLEN MASON

Sheffield 1981

1 | The Phenomenon of Touch

℞ Hugging, 4 times daily
Cuddling, take as necessary

If the reader were to be given a prescription such as this by his General Practitioner, he might be forgiven for thinking that the whole fabric of the National Health Service was beginning to crumble; he might consider it to be fun but not proper medical care. But Hanning (1980), reporting from a recent medical conference in Toronto, stated that four hugs per day acted as an antidote for depression; eight hugs put one well on the way to achieving mental stability; twelve promoted real psychological growth. The notion that personal contact may have an important part to play in the provision and maintenance of well being is intriguing and one that we intend to develop later in this book. This is one of the ways in which we wish to reconsider and re-evaluate the act of touching, and its effect on our lives.

Why the phenomenon of touch? We wish in this chapter to draw attention to the ubiquity of touching behaviour among humans; to the many occasions and contexts which elicit a touching response; to the endless variety of ways in which, for a multiplicity of purposes, we touch one another; yet still further to an infinity of intentions expressed and meanings understood by these actions, and no less to the constraints in the form of widely or narrowly accepted social rules which control the practice of touching within cultures and groups of people. Phenomenon, therefore, refers to the recognisable act of touching and to the experience of being touched. At the same time we use this word to question the apparent simplicity and straightforwardness of touching; to imply knowledge and yet some uncertainty of its causes and effects; and to establish that, in the final instance, the reality of physical contact is unique to each individual located in that space and that time.

Some of the examples of touching that follow are chosen to illustrate these ideas, as well as to challenge our easy and sometimes rather passive acceptance of actions that are both complex and powerful in their effect.

Everyday Idiom

Language, for us, provides the medium through which we try to give organisation and meaning to the world in which we live. It communicates our experience to others and allows us, in turn, to share their experiences. It is from our language that we get the first glimmerings of the importance that touch has for us. Man's external senses are generally described as being sight, hearing, taste, smell and touch. If we look in the Oxford English Dictionary we discover that touch occupies a staggering twenty-three columns spread over eight pages. This is considerably more than the entries for the remaining senses; sight, for example, is contained in only eleven columns, while smell rates a mere five. Although it can be argued that many of the terms do not describe *acts* of physical contact, this merely enhances the claim that the process of touching has come to acquire a symbolic as well as a practical significance. These phrases have become so entrenched in our everyday speech that we use them even though they indicate a contact removed from actual experience.

For example, we might read of a footballer, who, because of his involvement in a particular game, is described as having regained his 'touch', while a colleague appeared unable to 'get to grips' with the match and was thought to have 'lost his touch'. In racquet games such as tennis or squash we recognise that there are competitors who by virtue of their delicate 'stroking' and placing of the ball, are 'touch' players. The term 'out of touch' is much used to denote a person who does not seem to know what is happening around him or one who lost 'contact' with friends or relatives.

As members of an audience at a play or a film, we may be watching a performance that the critics will describe as 'gripping', that 'holds' us spellbound and 'plucks' at our emotions. Touch is also used to acknowledge illness, for when we suffer a mild form of influenza, we say 'I think I have a "touch" of flu'; or about an elderly relative 'She does not get about so well nowadays, she has a "touch" of arthritis.' We use these words in a way that once suggested the actual visitation of a particularly malevolent demon who physically put his evil hands upon us, affecting our bodies adversely. Mental problems share the same imagery for it is common to hear the expression 'a bit touched' of someone who is disturbed or acts in an odd way. We are apt to think of other people as being 'stand-offish', as 'keeping themselves to themselves', or being 'thick-skinned'. When they are irritable we call them 'touchy'. Some of them may be approachable and easily influenced – 'soft touches', while others are so isolated and inward-turning that the world fails to make any 'impression' on them.

These are examples of the ways in which the idea of contact is used to describe experiences. However, the point to be noted is that touching has become so much a part of verbal imagery that we take it very much for granted.

Intimate Touch
Of all the forms of sensory communication, touch is perhaps the only one that requires some kind of contract between the parties concerned. After all, we can look at or listen to another person, either openly or secretly, whenever we want; but to lay hands on someone's body needs permission or at least acquiescence if it is to be personally or socially acceptable. Whatever the reason for the contact may be, it remains

an intrusion and a violation of personal space. In our society, actual physical contact as a full and free expression of intimacy is seen to occur only in two groups of people – between mothers and children and between lovers. This is not to deny that there is contact between other groups, so much as to emphasise the fact that they are more rigidly controlled by rules and conventions.

In the mother/child relationship, the physical intimacy that is developed is essential to the physiological and psychological growth of the infant and is a subject that we will refer to throughout the book. But, although this contact is one that perhaps is regarded as being an integral part of motherhood, it was once considered inadvisable to encourage it, since babies would only become spoilt if they were picked up too often. The fact that intimate body contact was the starting point of all loving relationships was either unrealised or disregarded.

That touch is also an expression of loving and caring is true of the adult human, especially between lovers, and here, of course, we are concerned with more physiologically mature mechanisms and a wider range of experience. It has been said that the skin is a genital organ in itself and it is true that many cultures have sought to increase the enjoyment and effectiveness of sexual activities through devices and strategies centred on stimulation of the skin and a heightening of tactile responses. One has only to read the *Kama Sutra** or *The Perfumed Garden*† to discover manoeuvres that reflect this, and are a tribute to man's ingenuity as well as his athletic ability.

Sexual 'pleasures' rely heavily on an increase in the stimulation of the skin, ranging from a quest for physical pain through beating, whipping or spanking, to the delicate

**Kama Sutra (Vatsyayana)* Trans: Sir R. Burton
  & F. F. Arbuthnot   Panther 1963
†*The Perfumed Garden (Nefzawi)* Trans: Sir R. Burton
  Panther 1967

pattes d'araignée, a tickling erotic massage using the lightest possible touch (Comfort 1975).

There has been, in recent years, a rapid increase in the number of massage parlours and visiting massage services that have sprung up all over the country. It is generally accepted, although it may not be true of every establishment, that there is an emphasis on the more sexual expressions of massage and that their main purpose is to provide sexual gratification either through massage or from other tactually stimulating services. Farley (1978) investigated a number of such massage parlours in America and came to the conclusion that 'Although explicit sexual considerations seem to be the major perceived *raison d'être* of massage parlors, the importance of the contribution of massage parlors to affectational factors, such as physical considerations of relaxation, etc., is almost equally emphasised by the masseuses'.

In our culture, we have come to believe that experiences of body contact fall into one or other of the groups that have been mentioned, ie, mother/child; lover/lover. In adults, therefore, any search for touching either as a giver or a receiver implies some commitment to sexual intercourse itself, even though it may be an expression of affection or care. This has led to an inhibition of touching particularly among females, based on the supposition that 'decent' girls do not allow such liberties. Hollender *et al.* (1969), however, has reported that in order to obtain the close body contact or embracing needed by some women, they were prepared to trade sexual intercourse as the price for being held and cuddled. In a later study, Hollender (1970) stated that women usually separate their wish for sexual satisfaction from their wish to be held but are willing to use what Hollender calls 'sexual enticement and seduction' in order to satisfy their skin 'hunger'. Culture has an influence on this subject because each one will give to its people a different level of tactile response. Huang *et al.* (1976) found . . . 'that cultural as well as psychological forces exert a profound influence on the wish to be held'.

But we should be aware that in terms of the amount of contact that occurs within the cultures that we know, there is a wide range of practices from total, free and uninhibited touching, to cultures almost totally devoid of contact. We realise from common knowledge that there are these differences and make value judgements about the level of tactility of any particular cultural, racial or ethnic group. For instance, we generally think of the Latin races as being highly committed to touching others, if only when we comment disparagingly on the bottom-pinching predeliction of the Italian male. The Anglo-Saxon personality seems to show the opposite tendency, for we tend to think of it as being more aloof, stand-offish and distant, at least in its tactile behaviour.

Jourard (1966) observed pairs talking in coffee shops in several countries and counted the number of times one person touched another. He found that the contacts ranged from 180 per hour in Puerto Rico, to none at all in London.

According to Montagu (1977) there are great differences in the amount of contact that children receive between what he calls the non-literate societies such as the Eskimo and Bushman and the more technologically-advanced societies like our own which are less inclined to demonstrate their feelings in this physical way.

More extreme, or perhaps simply unusual, descriptions of touching behaviour are found in the literary accounts of the Marquis de Sade. Here the attitudes of the sexual aggressor (usually male) allow little for the feelings and autonomy of those subjected (usually female). Indeed, many of the sexual acts related in De Sade's *Memoirs* are horrifyingly brutal and callous, involving sexual exploitation and a degree of physical violence unmatched by what sells as pornographic literature today. The word 'sadism' originally implying sexual satisfaction from inflicting or watching cruelty has lost something of its force today particularly in its adjectival form. Still the question is raised. What is the significance of these stories? What is (or was) there in man that he, at least in fantasy, needs to express himself or be stimulated in such an extreme fashion?

D. H. Lawrence, on the other hand, whose literary ability and sensitivity enabled him to exalt simultaneously both the physical and spiritual reality of sexual contact, as for example in *Lady Chatterly's Lover*, tells of an unexpected liaison between sister and adopted brother all turning on a caress in the short story entitled *You Touched Me*. Matilda, preoccupied and anxious about her sick father, visits his bedroom late at night, forgetting that he was moved downstairs and that her brother Hadrian is sleeping in her father's bed.

' . . . her fingers met the nose and the eyebrows, she laid a fine delicate hand on his brow. It seemed fresh and smooth . . . A sort of surprise stirred her, in her entranced state. But it could not awaken her.' The incident aroused both persons' feelings and one wonders whether Matilda, in spite of her propriety, subconsciously wanted to be in Hadrian's room.

' . . . Hadrian too slept badly . . . the soft straying tenderness of her hand was on his face startled something out of his soul. He was a charity boy, aloof and more or less at bay. The fragile exquisiteness of her caress startled him most, revealed unknown things to him.' Could any instance of such a fleeting touch be so massively symbolic? Yet in reality it is sometimes surprising how critical human contact may be, especially in early childhood.

Seitz (1950) reports the case of a two-and-a-half-year-old girl referred by a dermatologist for psychiatric study of her hair loss. When feeding with a bottle the little girl reached for her scalp with her free hand and, by twisting and pulling, removed a clump of hair which she then conveyed to her lips and nose, tickling herself by brushing these hairs against this part of her face. The behaviour occurred only whilst feeding.

An extensive investigation revealed the facts that breast feeding had been abruptly stopped two weeks after birth, that a very punitive toilet training regime was instituted at

eighteen months, after which the child refused to eat solids
and regressed to bottle feeding. Dr Seitz reasoned that the
hair pulling might somehow be related to the baby's earlier
feeding patterns and that the breast experience tended to
alleviate the child's anxiety, particularly in respect of the
hairy stimulus around the nose and mouth. He then discovered that the mother's nipples were each surrounded by a
circle of hair. When a specially constructed teat with a
similar circle of human hair was fitted to the bottle the hair
pulling immediately ceased. This remarkable case study is a
singular reminder of the sensitivity of the neonate to skin
contact – a point we shall take up in Chapter 3.

The circumstances surrounding a recently reported case
(*Sunday Times* 4 May 1980), though less bizarre, are almost
as compelling. A nineteen-year-old borstal boy with 'a string
of convictions for theft' was allowed out, as part of a special
scheme to work in a hospital for the mentally handicapped
where he formed a caring friendship with a man ten years
older and severely handicapped. A feature of this relationship is that the handicapped man, Billy, likes to hug his
helper and to be hugged by him in return. In this action
there is an immediacy that cuts through many of the barriers
that might otherwise separate two people of such different
backgrounds and abilities. Each is able to express and fulfill
a need simultaneously and in a perfectly natural and spontaneous way.

Touch in other contexts

Obviously there are an enormous number of situations in
which humans touch each other for less intimate reasons, or
for practical rather than expressive purposes. Because these,
too have their own special character and meaning we will
illustrate them with some of the more representative examples.

Touch is used by most of us in ritual form to indicate the
relationship existing between one person and another.
Morris (1978) considers there are fourteen such indicators

which he calls 'body-contact tie signs'. These are:

1 Shaking hands
2 Guiding, using light pressure on the recipient's body
3 Patting, eg. as congratulations or greetings
4 Arm link
5 Shoulder embrace
6 Full embrace or hug
7 Hand in hand ·
8 Waist embrace
9 Kiss
10 Hand to head
11 Head to head
12 Caress
13 Body support
14 Mock attack

Whilst one can generally ascribe a level of intimacy or a type of relationship by observing episodes in which these forms are used it is still the case that there is considerable variation in the experience of any one of them. Shaking hands may imply that company is recognised and joined, but within this there are opportunities to signal warmth and cordiality, purpose or good faith, to be insistent or indifferent, accepting or demanding. The free hand is sometimes added to the clasp or to the other person's shoulder to enhance the engagement and to amplify the message.

Holding, striking, lifting, sharing the weight of another's body are some of the ways we use to communicate artistic ideas, to entertain, to compete or generally to recreate. Dancing, for example, has a long and quite exalted history in all its forms and today's popular dancing is no less an expression of contemporary culture, individual personality and group harmony than ever it was. It is worth reflecting on the fact that the waltz was once thought to be indecent when today, in a society much more permissive of sexual contact, the dancers often are apart.

By contrast, the kind of contact made in hand-to-hand combat and in many competitive sports represents an aggressive, challenging attitude and constancy of purpose, as well as skill and strength enough to achieve this. The human touch under these circumstances ranges from delicately incisive to crushingly powerful, and from bruising to lethal. Wrestling in its various forms relies totally on body contact and judo is so vitally concerned with the sensing of subtle changes in muscular tension and body balance in one's opponent that many blind people are successful even against sighted opposition.

The popularity of sports like boxing, where the objective is to strike an opponent as hard and often as possible and thus to render him incapable of continuing, is indeed testimony to the ideals of combat, more than to its experience. Similarly, the inescapable toughness of rugby league football is well explained by David Storey in *This Sporting Life*. The body is a machine of muscle and bone required to tackle, scrummage, ruck and maul (all technical terms, yet having their own descriptive force of the body in contact), as the situation demands, without much heed to injury or the vulnerability of mere tissue. Terkel (1977) catches the professional essence so necessary for the big money competitors in an interview with an ice hockey player: 'If you get hit, you get hit – with impersonal force. The guy'll hit you as hard as he can. If you get hurt the other players switch off. Nobody's sympathetic. When you get hurt the players don't look at you, even players on your own team.'

In this chapter we have tried to sketch out the width and depth of the business of human touching, as well as to question and perhaps provoke. It is appropriate, therefore, finally to consider the implications of the instruction from the *Carmelite Manual*, quoted by Bernstein (1976), which states that nuns should 'Touch no-one and do not allow yourself to be touched by anyone without necessity or evident reason, however innocent.'

2 | The Mechanisms of Touch

This chapter deals mainly with the skin, so perhaps the first thing that we should do is ask the question. What is the skin? Man has a tendency to take his body and its mechanisms for granted, giving it scant attention, at least while it is functioning reasonably well. After all, it is not often that we think deeply about our pancreas or our left elbow and, really, there is little reason to do so in the normal course of events. The skin is no exception and we only notice when it itches, produces a rash or erupts in unsightly blemishes. Other people, however, take more heed of our skin, for it may be regarded as being that part of ourselves which we put on show to the world, and although we might not consider that this 'outside' person is the real 'inside' self that we experience, but only a corporeal representation, nevertheless it is a shell that enables our fellow men to recognise and to some extent, judge and categorise us.

The skin, or more technically the integument, covers, in the adult an area of some 18,000 square centimetres, extending over the surface of the body and folding inwards to become continuous with the mucous linings of the urogenital, alimentary and respiratory tracts. Although the skin does form a complete covering for the body, it would be misleading to consider it as only a fitted and flexible bag designed for the sole purpose of constraining the more important parts of the body, keeping, as it were, one's insides inside. The skin is a complex and sophisticated organ, vital to our physiological survival; it acts as an active communicating bridge between the environment and the internal systems of the body, providing physical contact with the reality which is other than self.

Having said that the skin is more than a rather large carrier bag, and in view of its importance to the contents of this book, we will look first at its functions and then at its structure.

The Functions of the Skin

The skin can be said to have three broad functions:

1   it protects the internal structures and resists any invasive attempt to disturb the constancy of the internal environment in which the cells function;
2   it provides a metabolic and a storage facility; and
3   it acts as a vast sensory and communication network.

In spite of the innumerable changes that take place in the external world, the body, through many compensatory mechanisms, seeks to provide an unvarying internal state. If this state alters by any significant amount for any reason, then the organism will be at risk. This regulation is termed homeostasis and is necessary if the organism is to remain independent of the often unpredictable changes in the external environment. The skin, because it provides the body's boundary, becomes the first barrier against attacks from mechanical, thermal or chemical agencies. The outer layer, the epidermis, has low properties of permeability and so retards the passage of toxic material, while hyaluronic acid contained within the deeper layer, the dermis, further acts as a barrier, particularly to bacterial infection. Sebum, the product of glands in the skin is thought to have bacteriostatic and fungistatic properties. But while the skin acts to prevent or minimise the intrusion of foreign substances, it also limits the outward passage of fluids. The low permeability of the dermis combined with the water binding properties of hyaluronic acid help to regulate fluid loss, thus maintaining tissue hydration and preventing undue desiccation.

The skin contains a vascular network which is capable of storing 4·5% of the total blood volume. The capabilities of this system far exceed the needs of the skin itself and so it serves the entire body in the control of blood pressure and in conjunction with the sweat glands, in the regulation of body temperature. While these mechanisms do not represent the entire capability of the body's protective power, they do indicate the role that the skin plays in enabling the organism to retain, maintain or regain the homeostasis that is essential for the efficient functioning of its cells and ultimately for its survival.

The skin produces compounds which, when they are exposed to ultraviolet radiation that is contained in the normal atmosphere, synthesise vitamin D. The skin is involved in steroid metabolism and it also participates in the formation of active hormones derived from steroid precursors from the blood and in the regulation of the activity of some steroid hormones.

Because of those factors contained in the dermis and epidermis, the skin is able to store fluid: it is capable of storing from 18% to 20% of the total water in the body. We are also aware of its ability to store fat. Again, while we have not mentioned every metabolic and storage activity, the examples used serve to remind us that the skin is an active participant in the functioning of the body rather than being a sleeping partner.

Of particular significance to this book is the skin's provision of a mechanism by which the organism receives information from and transmits it to, the outside world. We have already noted that we use the skin to recognise those superficial characteristics that typify a particular individual; further, we come to realise that it constitutes an organ of expression which is capable of revealing feelings, intentionally or unintentionally.

The skin represents a complex system that receives information through a network of different receptor organs, information which must be continuous if the brain is to interpret and evaluate the changes taking place in the external environment in a way that permits protection and maintenance of homeostasis and provides the means by which the individual can make sense of those elements lying outside his personal boundary.

The Structure of the Skin

The skin is essentially a veneered structure, comprising two distinct layers: the superficial one, the epidermis, is a non-vascular stratified entity whose cells are constantly being shed, flaked-off by the action of the weather and clothing. Below this lies a fibro-elastic dermis which contains the blood vessels, glands and hair follicles and which provides the new cells to replace those lost from the surface of the body. The junction between these two layers is distinctive in Man in that it exhibits a series of ridges and folds which serve to lock them together and prevent loss of continuity through shearing forces.

The deeper-placed dermis is a tough, flexible layer and constitutes from 15–20% of the total body weight. It is not uniform throughout the body, being thicker on the palms of the hands and the soles of the feet and on the posterior and medial sides of the body. Consisting of connective tissue with some non-striated muscle fibres, it encloses the vessels and is usually described as having two layers, a deeper reticular and a more superficial papillary.

The presence of the protein material collagen in the reticular layer provides it with a remarkable resistance to mechanical stress. The elastic fibres which are also present are thought to be responsible for the restoration of the collagen network after it has been distorted. The fibres are arranged in rows rather like bundles of drinking straws, so that if they are split longitudinally by a sharp object such as a knife the individual fibres are forced apart rather than cut and so there is minimal scar formation as the wound heals. If, however, the cut is made, as it were, across the grain, then much more scarring will be found. This is significant when considering the direction of a surgical incision if the presence and amount of scar tissue is of particular importance. In the limbs these bundles form the cleavage lines and run longitudinally with respect to the member, while in the trunk they are horizontal. Fibres subjected to prolonged stretching fail to regain their original length and the results of this can be seen as the stretch marks common after pregnancy or intensive weight reduction.

The papillary layer contains the sensitive vascular structures, the papillae. Each papillus consists of connective tissue carrying a capillary loop, nerve fibres and sensory endings. The papillae are arranged in a pattern of parallel lines which fit neatly into indentations on the under surface of the epidermis. Because the epidermis has no blood vessels nutriments can diffuse through the papillae, the indentations bringing them into more intimate contact. The ridges formed by the pattern result in loops and whorls that are visible on the surface of the skin, these being familiar to most people as fingerprints.

Blood enters the skin through tiny arteries which pass from the underlying tissues to form a plexus or network at the junction between the dermis and the fascia below. After supplying the hair follicles and glands, a further plexus is formed between the two layers of the dermis. Capillaries course through the papillae then loop back to drain into a series of venous plexuses. Normally, blood passes through the arteries, arterioles and capillaries before returning via the venules and veins. The skin, however, demonstrates a system in which the blood flows directly from artery to vein with no intermediate vessels involved; this serves to regulate the temperature throughout the body and provide control of blood pressure.

Lymph vessels are present in great numbers and communicate at all levels. They filter back plasma proteins that have seeped into the tissues and also remove particulate matter from them. Within the dermis lie the structures generally described as being appendages of the skin, that is the nails, hair and glands.

The nails, which are only to be found in the primates, are flattened flexible plates of keratin. They form a rigid support for the pads of the digits and in the case of the hand, they enable the fingers to pick up tiny objects and to hold them. Because of this function they must be considered as playing a part in the tactile mechanism.

Hairs are found in nearly every part of the body with the exception of the palms and soles, the nail area and parts of of the external genitalia. Hair differs greatly in texture, length and colour but may be divided into three groups. These are:

1   lanugo or downy hairs which cover the limbs, back and parts of the face;
2   long, soft hairs which cover the face as beard or moustache, the scalp, axillae and pubic region; and
3   stiff hairs found as eyebrows, eyelashes and in the ear and nose.

Each hair follicle has attached to it a small smooth muscle which receives a nerve supply from the sympathetic nervous system and which, when it is stimulated, contracts and produces the phenomenon known as 'goose pimples'. The hair acts as a protection against minor dysfunction; the eyebrows, for instance, direct sweat away from the eyes.

Sebaceous glands are unique to the mammals and are most numerous in Man, They are most abundant on the face and scalp but absent on the palms and soles. The glands have no direct exit on to the surface of the skin but discharge their secretion into a hair follicle. This secretion, which is the result of the decomposition of the glands' own cells, is called sebum and acts as a natural lubricant, preventing damage from excessive drying or moisture. However, it has been stated (Montagna & Parakkal 1974) that the real function of sebum would seem to be that of a pherome* and that it provides the scent that distinguishes one person from another.

Sweat glands are found all over the body and are of large size in the axillae and ano-genital areas. Especially numerous on the palms and soles, the glands open on the surface of the skin as pores on the top of the papillary ridges. The secretion which we know as perspiration aids in the reduction of body temperature as it evaporates from the skin. Sweating is also a feature of the response to stress, pain, sexual activity or general emotional arousal. Indeed, the sweating response is so sensitively linked to psychological arousal that it is used as a physiological index of this state. Sweating affects the electrical conductivity of the skin, and the resistance may be measured simply by attaching surface electrodes to the body, say to the index and fourth fingers. This process is the basis of the so-called 'lie detector', once much used in the USA; it is also employed as a measure of stress, both for research and remedial purposes.

Embryologically, the epidermis is derived from the ectoderm along with practically the whole of the nervous system, including the cranial and spinal ganglia and the sympathetic ganglia of the autonomic nervous system. This relationship between the skin and the nervous system has provoked the comment (Montagu 1977) that:

'It would, therefore, improve our understanding of these matters if we were to think of the skin as the external nervous system, an organ which from its earliest differentiation remains in intimate association with the internal or central nervous system.'

The epidermis, like the dermis, is a stratified structure possessing a deeper germinative zone and a more superficial corneal zone. From the deep layer the cells gradually find their way towards the surface of the skin; changing shape

*Pherome This is a chemical substance by which insects and animals recognise each other and the tracks used by others of their kind.

as they do so, becoming somewhat flatter and also losing their nuclei. At the corneal or horny zone the cells, now anuclear and filled with the protein keratin, tend to flake

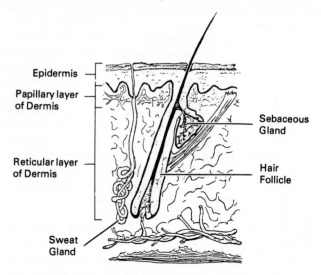

Epidermis

Papillary layer
of Dermis

Sebaceous
Gland

Reticular layer
of Dermis

Hair
Follicle

Sweat
Gland

Fig 1   The skin

away and be lost to the body. Figure 1 shows these two zones.

When we look at this outer surface of the body it is obvious that it presents a varying cover. There are bumps and hollows, areas covered with hair, differences of colour and of texture. It is also clear that the skin is not entirely smooth but is scored, lined and wrinkled in a number of ways which presents to the world a changing map of experience, emotion and achievement. They say, this is me and this is my life. Perhaps the most hated of these lines are the wrinkles that are the inevitable consequence of the ageing process and which are caused by the gradual loss of elasticity in the fibres of the dermis.

If we take the hand as an example, we can see on the

palm a number of well-defined creases. Whether these lines have, as it is claimed astrological significance, we do not know, but we can say that they represent those regions where the skin is firmly bound down to the underlying tissues and that they indicate the position of the joints. Termed flexure lines, they can be seen in other areas of the body, for instance at the back of the knee or in the crook of the elbow.

On a close inspection of the pads of the fingers, a series of parallel looped lines is visible. This pattern, also to be seen on the same portion of the toes, is remarkably regular and consistent. It relates to the formation of the dermal papillae and is unique to any individual. In 1823 J. E. Purkinje published a paper in which he demonstrated that these 'friction ridges' could be divided into nine different types. Attempts were made to use this knowledge in the identification of individuals but it was only at the end of the 19th century that a comprehensive system was devised. This was the work of Sir Edward Henry, Chief Commissioner of Scotland Yard, and was published as *Classification and Uses of Fingerprints*. The Henry system, as it was called, was adopted officially in 1901. As a means of identification, fingerprinting forms a nearly perfect method. It has been calculated that the lowest computed odds against any two people producing an identical print are 67,000,000,000 to 1.

The tension lines of the skin appear as a network of intersecting lines dividing the surface into tiny diamond-shaped areas. While they do correspond to variations in the pattern of the fibres of the dermis, the relationship is not as clear as it is in the pads of the fingers.

The final colour of the skin is determined by the blending of at least five different elements, the pigments Melanin, Melanoid and Carotene and by haemoglobin and oxyhaemoglobin in the blood. The enormous variation in skin colour seen in the different races of the world reflects the amount of melanin that is present in the skin. Complete absence of pigment is sometimes found in an individual; this true 'white skin' is termed albinism and may occur in any racial type. The skin has a rich nerve supply, the cranio-spinal and autonomic systems supplying both myelinated and non-myelinated fibres* Sensory nerve endings that are present have been described in a number of ways by different authorities but in this book they will be considered as they are in Gray's Anatomy (35th edition). For the purposes of this text, however, we can deal only with the exteroceptors; these are nerve endings which respond to the multitude of stimuli and changes in the external environment and which are placed on or very near to the skin.

Exteroceptors can be broadly divided into:

1   the very specific sensory endings associated with vision, hearing, taste and smell; and
2   the more general endings found in the skin and around the hair follicles which exhibit as free nerve-endings or as corpuscular organs.

Free nerve-endings are found in all types of connective tissue, including the dermis, meninges, joint capsules and bone. The fibres which carry impulses from the periphery are of small diameter, have low conduction speeds and require a greater stimulus to activate them than do the larger nerves. Their functional significance cannot be stated with complete certainty but it has been suggested that they act as a monitoring mechanism that constantly reviews the fluctuating state of the environment.

The second type of general receptor is the corpuscular-end organ, of which there are several distinct types, which although they differ in many ways share the common feature of having a capsule which encloses the terminal portion. Traditionally, these have been associated with the investigators who first described them and so we meet in

---

*Myelinated nerves are those which are sheathed in a white, fat-like substance called myelin. Fibres which have no myelin sheath are termed non-myelinated.

texts such names as the tactile corpuscles of Meissner, the lamellated corpuscles of Pacini, the bulbous corpuscles of Krause and the tactile discs of Merkel. A specific form of sensation such as pressure, temperature, etc. has been attributed sometimes to each of these nerve endings but there is some scepticism over this viewpoint and it has been suggested that appreciation of the different types of sensation depends rather more on the pattern and arrangement of the impulses arriving at the sensory cortex of the brain (Melzack & Wall 1962).

It is clear that there are differences in the sensitivity of various parts of the body. In the adult we might place the hand as the most sensitive part, but in the baby the region of the greatest tactile significance is the mouth and the lips. We use our hands very much as gatherers of sensory information, because we are dexterous enough to manipulate objects. The child, however, lacks this facility when it is very young and so it tends to use that area which is richest in sensations; consequently the child moves everything towards its mouth as a preliminary assessment of its use. It is hard to put in any sort of order those regions of the body that are more sensitive and those which are less so, but at brain level these differences in sensitivity are shown by the size of representation on the sensory cortex, for as the function of a part becomes involved in activities of increasing complexity its area of representation on the brain becomes correspondingly larger. The disproportion in body sensation is described using the sensory *manikin* and it is clear from Figure (2) overleaf that the lips and hands cover a large area.

Signals from the nerve-endings in the skin are transmitted through the sensory ganglia to the posterior columns of the spinal cord and thence via the postero-ventral nuclei of the thalamus to the post-central gyrus (a gyrus being a convolution of the brain) situated in the parietal lobe of the brain. The anterior part of this area receives all the information from the skin while the posterior part relates the sensations to past experience so that the individual is able to recognise them. For example, when an object is held in the hand or stroked, it can be identified by this means alone and does not need the aid of vision. There has been mention (Keele-Neil 1961) of a second somatic area which has been discovered but as yet there is no clear notion of its role.

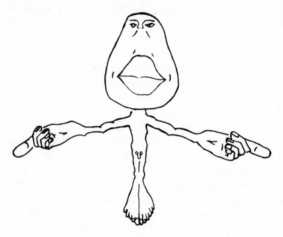

Fig 2   The sensory body of man, drawn to a scale indicated by the area of representation of each part of the brain

Sensation and Perception

When we use the term sensation, therefore, we refer primarily to this process of information transmission from the sensory nerve endings through the nervous system to the brain. It identifies the existence of some energy change at the periphery of the body and the translating of an impulse. Sensation can be assumed in the reflex response to a pin prick or the slightest touch with a feather and there are many sources giving evidence of psycho-physiological thresholds at which stimuli are just detected (see, for example, Hilgard *et al.* 1971).

Perception on the other hand is much more complex. It

calls into being the whole of the thinking, remembering and analytical nature of Man. The sensory information is arranged and synthesised in such a way as to give it the most meaning in the circumstances of the moment and in the accumulated experience of the individual.

Essentially, perception involves an act of selection-interpretation. In daily living a great deal of information is always available: the enviroment alters, people move about and communicate, noises impinge upon other noises. We have a tendency to attend only to those things that have some value or meaning at any one time: the pressure of our buttocks on the chair, the touch of the page against our hand, pass unnoticed unless we consciously make an effort to think of these sensations.

When several people receive exactly the same sensory stimulus we can assume that it will impinge itself on sensory nerve endings in precisely the same way, that is, the physiological response will be constant for each person. The interpretation of that impulse, however, will not be so. The impulses become changed in some way as they pass through the various relays in the nervous system to a point where the pattern of impulses that are represented at the sensory cortex will differ significantly from those originally transmitted from the periphery. As an example of this, the Rorschach ink-blot test is used to diagnose mental states. The black shape is interpreted differently by each client and this in turn is interpreted in symptomatic terms by the psychiatrist. Our perception of any object depends on a number of features which will be discussed in detail in the next chapter in their relationship to human touch.

Broadly speaking, there are two sets of factors that affect the perceptive process, one external to the perceiver and the other internal to him. The surroundings or context within which perception takes place helps to determine what is actually experienced. For instance, a commonly used trick places the the word 'the' at the end of one line and at the beginning of next as well (see above) ; this is not expected by the general reader and will only normally be noticed by proof-readers or those whose attention is directed to expect it. As another example, the interpretation of a simple gesture such as placing a hand on another person's shoulder will vary depending on the situation and the persons involved. Totally different meanings will be attributed to the gesture as performed by a doctor, a tailor or a policeman. This contextual interpretation of touch is important in the field of therapy and will be discussed later in the book.

The classic experiments of Asch (1956) illustrate how the opinions and actions of other people affect perception and offer clues and guides to the interpretation of what is taking place. One person was required to make a simple judgement about the length of a line – in fact to say which of the three given comparison lines it was equal to. In a group of people apparently similar to himself all of whom were asked to make the judgement he found that the others chose a line different from his own choice. These people were accomplices of the experimenter, merely following his instructions. Six or seven of every group of ten put in this position came up with wrong choices, being affected by the false judgements given by the others.

Some effects are cultural. The society in which we are raised, to an extent, determines how we understand and interpret certain aspects of the environment. Young children often find worms to be interesting playthings; they enjoy handling them and do not appear to be deterred by the feel of the soft, squirming creatures. After a few years, however, the children, especially girls, begin to exhibit the elaborate revulsion that adults tend to display in similar circumstances.

Our perceptions are also affected by internal considerations such as our past experiences and our current needs. That past experience dictates what we see, hear, feel or otherwise sense should not be altogether surprising since at the heart of most professional training lies the notion that certain types of perceptual response should be attained from particular collections of signs and symptoms. The past experience of the professional leads him to interpret the evidence for dysfunction in a limited number of ways which, if his training has been effective, will usually bring him to agree with the opinions of other 'experts' who have similar experience.

Basic human needs contribute to our perception, for it changes depending on whether we are hungry or thirsty, aggressive or in need of companionship, secure or bored.

As an example of the highly specialised and individualistic nature of perception in humans, we will consider the nature of pain. Although in general the nature and degree of pain felt depends upon the type and intensity of the stimulus, like other sensory stimuli it is interpreted according to the situation and the circumstances. It is affected by culture, experience, personality and personal differences in sug-gestibility and anxiety. It was noted (Beecher 1959) that only one in three of the Second-World-War soldiers wounded on the Anzio beachhead required morphine for their injuries whereas comparably 'wounded' civilian surgical cases re-quired morphine in four out of five cases. Presumably the meaning of the injury was sufficiently different in the two groups; the wounds for the soldiers possibly constituted the envied 'Blighty' one, signifying an end to the anxiety and trauma of combat and a withdrawal to the relative comfort and safety of hospital. For the civilians, it meant withdrawal from the comforts of home life to the relative discomfort and anxiety of the hospital.

Cultural factors also affect the way that pain is per-ceived. Melzack (1977), in *The Puzzle of Pain*, describes an Amerindian ritual in which the celebrant swings on two ropes attached to his body by hooks thrust into the muscles of his lower back. At the climax of the ceremony the entire body weight is taken on these hooks yet the man shows none of the normal signs of pain: rather, he is in a state of exultation.

Tolerance to pain seems to be greater with extraversion. It has been shown (Bond 1971) that people who are less emotional and more sociable, experience little pain when in hospital for surgery, whilst those in opposite categories feel rather more. These are, of course, generalised findings and do not imply that all extroverts and phlegmatic people have less pain than those who are introverted or anxious. It would appear that some people are more suggestible than others. With appropriate preparation, various forms of treatment such as the use of placebos, acupuncture anaesthesia, or the laying-on of hands, may have the effect of lessening pain, especially when there is no obvious mechanical basis for its presence. In a similar way, the result of giving information about future pain or discomfort has shown (Janis 1971; Haywood 1975) that such information given pre-operatively and inducing moderate levels of fear in surgical patients, acted as a kind of innoculation against the pain: these patients were both more comfortable and less emotional during convalescence.

This is not to imply that the use of psychological mechanisms in the treatment of patients is somehow second-rate or inferior to more definitive methods of relieving pain, or that there is something dishonest about choosing modes which 'pander' to the patient's apparent distortion of symptoms. Rather, we should be alerted by the fact that such mechanisms exist and we should neither ignore nor discard them, but make use of them when it is appropriate to do so.

The nature of our senses and what it means when we obtain information from the external world cannot be wholly explained in a mechanistic manner. We know that the structures which are described in textbooks of anatomy will be, with only minor variations, identical in all of us. Similarly, the nature of the nervous impulses and their mode of travel in the nervous system remains predictable. What, however, is evident is that the perception of what goes on is unique to the individual. We cannot say for certain what a particular sensation means to another person because we cannot sense or feel it for them. This theme is further explored in the next chapter – let us for the time being identify this isolation in the words of R. D. Laing (1975): 'I cannot experience your experience. You cannot experience my experience. We are both invisible men. All men are invisible to one another.'

3 | Developmental Aspects of Touch

In the womb, the unborn child lies totally enclosed and protected from the outside world. He is, at this point, physically a part of the mother, sharing as he does, the maternal circulation and taking support for his delicate body from the fluid-filled uterus. It is that same watery environment which transmits sensations to his skin, thus providing the first stimuli to his developing sensory mechnisms. He will become aware of the beat of his mother's heart and of the sensations generated by her movements and changes of position, but he will, however, remain a passive recipient of these stimuli for he cannot chose or explore them, nor can he ignore them. Here, for a brief time, he exists in a warm, secure world, his own garden of Eden.

The fetal brain grows rapidly, so much so that there is a danger that the skull, flexible though it is, will become too large to pass through the maternal pelvis. The child, therefore, must be born before this state is reached even though it will be at the expense of his physical and mental maturity. The human animal is not capable of running with the herd soon after birth and he will remain a helpless and immature creature for some considerable time. Why this should be so can be better understood if we think of the human gestation period as being in two halves. The first half covers the time spent in the womb and lasts for approximately nine months. The birth then occurs for the reason described above. The second half of gestation, therefore, takes place outside the womb and lasts at least until the child can crawl successfully, when it can be said to be physically disengaged from the mother. The infant, of course, is aware that there is a difference between these two phases and needs constant reminding that he is still in a world that is warm and safe, even if these qualities are no longer quite so immediate.

At birth itself, the child is subjected to a long period of intense and constant stimulation of his skin as he is expelled from the uterus. This provides, for him, a unique and unrepeatable experience, which, although apparently traumatic, is essential for his future well-being.

The relationship between stimulation of the skin and the arousal of essential body systems has been studied in animals. It is generally recognised that the elaborate licking that animals give to their young is more than a concern for cleanliness, for it provides the young with the stimuli that they require in order to activate the gastrointestinal and genitourinary systems. Without this licking, the young are unable to function properly and thus their chances of survival are lessened.

Man, it would appear, is the only animal that does not lick its young and it has been thought that the more intense stimulation that the process of labour induces serves the same purpose, that is, as a method of activating the infant's body systems in preparation for independent existence. If that first major sensory experience is denied to the child, as it is in Caesarian-delivered babies, or in premature babies where the stimulus is less pronounced, we must consider that this constitutes a disadvantage. Research has indicated that such infants show measurable differences from normally delivered babies in such items as biochemical levels, susceptibility to body system disorders, behavioural problems and emotional disturbances (Drillien 1959; Shirley 1939; Straker 1962).

The child will need to build up a healthy body image and the touching of his body by those close to him and by himself, enables him to do this. It is important to realise that the ego is identified with the body and that loss of one often means loss of the other. The schizophrenic, for example, appears unable to stay in the generally accepted objective world. A feature of this condition may be the unacceptability or unreality of his body.

Perceptual Systems

There are within the human organism more than the five traditional senses or perceptual systems of sight, hearing, smell, taste and touch that we ascribe to man. There are, for instance, perceptions of joint position, muscle tension and other internal states. Therefore the reader will be able to remind himself, without taking his eyes off the page, of the position and feel of his feet. This proprioceptive sense as it is called, represents the individual's positioning and movement to himself, in the same way that other sensory nerve endings inform of an empty stomach or a full bladder. However, man's senses are commonly listed as five for two reasons. One is that for most action and decision making at conscious levels these five are the most important – they have most significance in the struggle to survive, adapt to and thrive on the challenge offered by man's environment.

The second reason is that it is through these five senses that man is able to identify and exchange information about shared experiences. The distinction between internal and external receptor systems is, here, a significant one. While man's experience of his *internal* environment (ie. of his full stomach) is his and his alone – nobody else can experience what is happening inside his body – by contrast his experience of the world outside his body may be shared to a greater or lesser extent by others. Any account of his inner states is unverifiable in the terms in which it is given; descriptions of the environment around him, however, can be verified by others.

For example, only the mother is capable of sensing and interpreting the movements of the baby living inside her. Other mothers, of course, feel their babies moving about inside them, but these are different babies in different wombs at different times. In contrast, several people may experience the countryside as they walk through it together. They smell the honeysuckle and new-mown grass, they hear birds singing from an identical source at the same instant, they may each touch the moss on a stone wall or notice the reflections of trees overhanging the river. Several hundred people together may witness the same performance of a play and doubtless several hundreds of millions have the opportunity to follow the same events simultaneously during the Olympic Games with their eyes and ears directed towards identical images on television sets.

Thus the sharing of experience is commonly achieved through the senses of sight, sound, smell, taste and touch. Even these experiences, however, are common merely in so far as they originate in part from the reality of the physical world. One does not have to move entirely to an existentialist position to appreciate that every interpretation of this physical world is different from the next. No two people can perceive the same object in an *exactly* equivalent way, however alike they may be in background and other relevant ways. In the first place, one can never be physically in the same position as another person and, in the second, there can be no guarantee of any duplication of sensory or perceptual responses.

Furthermore, the possibility of identical experiences seems to vary somewhat between the various perceptual modes or senses. Visual and auditory perceptions of a given stimulus are, relatively speaking, immediate in comparing the stimulus input of two or more people, while the comparison of the same stimulus through the modes or smell, taste or touch will take longer as each person in turn gains a similar degree of proximity to the object. There is some paradox in this because the more immediate comparisons to be made are of those aspects of the environment that are physically further away. Thus we are quicker able to share an opinion or a statement about someone's appearance than we are about the warmth of that person's skin. In another sense, though, taste and touch are the most immediate of all our sensory modes. These systems deal with the nearest and most intimate relationships between the body and its physical surroundings. They respond in the most literal way to contact with other objects close to them. The young baby carries everything to his mouth in order to experience this quality. For the child, touching, clinging to playthings or its parents is the ultimate assurance of ownership, love and security. The importance of a child's physical contact with a parent-figure is a theme we shall return to later on.

Even the mature adult seems to have some need to closeness or contact with others in times of crisis or threat. One of the world's largest airlines has run a special course to help those people who have an incapacitating fear of flying to overcome their difficulty. During their first flight, these sufferers were encourage to obtain reasurance from each other by holding or embracing in moments of acute stress. The effectiveness of this action may depend on the security of the parental contact learned many years before. In other threatening situations, herding together and holding on to others may alleviate the physical threat through a belief in the safety of numbers or may obtain reassurance from the more competent or the more experienced members of the group.

Touch, therefore, is the most personal of the perceptual systems in terms both of its uniqueness or limitation to one individual and of its being the most intimate of the sensory experiences. We have said earlier that touch is the most basic of the senses: as this chapter attempts to show, it plays a vital part in the development of visual perception, it has a fundamental biological significance in the provision of security and nurture for the young, it acts as an increasingly subtle and sensitive medium of expression for communication with others, and, of course, continues throughout life as a means of primary experience of the physical environment, whether the actual purpose is investigatory, manipulatory or pleasure-seeking. Without it, one would almost literally be as a body lost in space.

Touch and Vision

The development of the perceptual systems does not take place in a piecemeal fashion; one mode does not develop independently from another. For example, the understanding of distance in space as indicated by visually received information must be reinforced in the early stages by reaching out to touch what is seen: thus we understand what is within reach and what is beyond reach. The baby explores his immediate surroundings in this way, developing what Piaget calls 'schemas' which enable him intellectually to represent in some coordinated way the relationships between himself and his environment. These schemas are really insights or ways of understanding the multiplicity of objects and events that exist in our world. According to Piaget, the formation and re-formation of these ways of structuring or representing the world proceeds in stages the attainment of which is indicative of our intellectual growth.

The intimate relationship of tactile experience and vision in the growth of the young organism has been well demonstrated in an experiment by the psychologists Held & Hein (1963). During the experiment, carried out in the early part of the lives of two kittens, visual experience was limited mainly to periods of exploration inside a controlled environment. The two animals were linked together by an arm which revolved about a point midway between them. While one of the two was merely harnessed to its end of the arm the other was cradled by a container out of contact with the ground. The first kitten, therefore was free to explore its environment within the limits of the 'roundabout', whilst the second kitten was simply a passenger whose visual experience, while broadly similar to that of his opposite number, was nonetheless out of his direct control: the passive kitten saw only what the active kitten allowed him to see. Later, when the kittens were removed from the apparatus and tested on their visual responses to various stimuli it was found that both had the normal capacity to see, but that only the active kitten seemed able to respond with movement to environmental stimuli that would evoke this: it appeared that for the visual input to be acted upon some experience of this action was necessary. Thus, the development of normal visual interpretation of events coupled with adaptive responses would seem to depend on having some tactile and kinesthetic input simultaneously with the visual perception.

Studies of children and adults who were blind from birth, but who at some later stage recovered their sight, usually by a surgical operation to remove cataracts from their eyes, reveal similar sorts of deficit in response. As Bower (1977) points out: 'If the condition is not corrected at an early age, it might as well not be corrected at all in the vast majority of cases. The correction may be a technical success, and optical success, but a complete functional failure. Generally, by the time a baby has lived six months without the benefit of patterned vision, it is too late to introduce patterned vision. The baby makes no use of it at all.' Bower refers to the classic cases described by Uhthoff in von Senden's book *Space and Sight* (1932): 'On being called to come the child at first stands still; only when bidden more firmly does she begin to grope her way forward, obviously directing herself by ear alone, though her eyes are wide open. Her line of advance is generally a wrong one, and she bumps into every obstacle.'

Von Senden's accounts of blind adults who regained their sight is in some respects even more distressing. Far from being the all-revealing, insightful experience that one might imagine for these handicapped people, the acquisition of sight left many of them weary and confused. There was a reluctance to employ the sensory information available, to interpret and to try to understand its meanings. The difference between being able to touch and often instantly identify and having to puzzle and strain to relate the new visual image to some tactually familiar object is well illustrated in the case of a young French man whose operation allowed him to see, but left him with 'no interest at all in acquiring new knowledge; he continued to behave like a blind man'. His sweetheart, also blind, made the following experiment with him: 'One day, during the vine harvest, she picked a bunch of grapes and showed it to her lover from a distance. "What is that?" she asked him; "It is dark, blue and shiny" (ie. purely qualitative features). "Anything else?" – "It isn't smooth, it has bumps and hollows." "Can one eat it?" – "I don't know." – "Then take it and try." As soon as he touched the bunch, he cried: "But they're grapes!" '

Thus, in newly-sighted people the sense of touch remains dominant: they try continually to replace visual impressions by tactile ones in order to recognise the object, but eventually will come to realise that the tactile schema obtained by tracing out the object's shape with the hand or the finger relates directly to the visual image, and a process of translation becomes possible. Similarly, the perception of space, previously impossible except in terms of successions of contacts or movements, is gradually acquired by progressive enlargement of the spatial field. The penetration of their subjective space and the location of objects at various depths within it are achieved only with concentration on the visual input and its relationship with immediate tactile experience. The linking of touch and vision, the coordination of hand and eye, seemingly so natural and normal for the sighted, occurs in von Senden's cases only with persistent and intelligent effort. It would appear that this late learning is nothing like as efficient as that which most of us achieve in the first few years of life.

The Integration of Touch and Other Senses

Gibson (1966) has used the term 'haptic system' to mean the 'sensibility of the individual to the world adjacent to his body by the use of his body'. Essentially, this is a perceptual system through which the child becomes literally in touch with the world, developing through his early tactile experiences his capacities for other sensory perceptions.

The ease with which we achieve a well-articulated response in dealing with the world in a number of sensory modes simultaneously is belied by the enormous amount of preparatory and developmental experience in the early years of life. Children undertake seemingly endless repetitions of various acts until they understand or come to terms with the features which interest them at this stage of their learning. Again, Piaget (1954) proposes that these understandings (schemas) are either reinforced or revised by the child's impressions of and actions on his world.

For example, from the time the very young baby first reaches out to encounter the fresh, strangely-textured, warm and cold world within his grasp, he begins to define two vitally important boundaries. One is that of his own body, sensorily endowed, as we have seen, with an appropriate density of fine nerve-endings, each of which informs him of some kind of change at that particular limit of his physical being; the other, of course, is the boundary of some objects of contact, whether it is part of the cot in which he lies, his mother's face or the clothes in which he is so snugly layered against the cold air.

As vision develops, this tactile and positional appreciation of his object world is gradually strengthened and added to by the *appearance* (ie. his visual appreciation) of the body-object relationship: he sees himself in contact; he perceives the possibility of negotiating contact with some object when it is near, even before such contact has occurred. When, by his own efforts, it does occur, another bridge has been built; another linking, confirmatory experience adds integrity to the evidence of his senses. The satisfaction on a baby's face on gaining such contact after a coordinated effort is obvious, even to the uninitiated.

Later, the pre-school child engages in a vast range of touching experiences which, in turn, serve a variety of purposes. One of these purposes is that of exploration and discovery of the quality of the substances and materials, both natural and artificial, encountered in the purposeful business of play. After repeated experiments, children come to an intimate understanding of the relationship between their own acts and the changes that take place apparently in consequence of these acts. For the child here is the original scientist trying to discover and employ the true nature of cause and effect in his participation in events close to him. An example will help to make the point more effectively. 'Suzanne spends twenty minutes at the sink. She fills one jug with water from the bowl and then uses this to fill a cup. When the cup is full she goes on filling the jug and pouring yet more water into the already full cup. The water flows over the sides of the cup onto her hand and back into the bowl. She is absorbed in the activity, apparently enjoying the sensations involved to the full: she sees, hears and feels the water; she is aware of its flow and its force from all these sources simultaneously; each sensation supplements and binds the others; her "understanding" depends on several modes of sensation, not least on touch. The shiny smoothness of the water is evident in its feel, its appearance and even in its flowing sound.' Here, Suzanne may be learning many things: about the physical properties of water and the capacities of the jug and the cup; about the means of controlling the movement of the water; even about the need to consider the actions of other children who share the play situation with her. But she is also responding aesthetically and emotionally to the experience, enjoying the sensuality of it and perhaps connecting this to other similar sensations, reviving previous emotions, linking these with particular words which she expressed out loud; or perhaps she hangs onto a single notion of slipperiness, smoothness or reflectivity, either just discovered or recalled from the impression of another liquid.

Touch as Primary Identification

The above example shows how the sense of touch provides

information which, when integrated with that from other sensory modes, enables intelligent learning about the world to take place. Obviously, this kind of tactile experience has a unique contribution in the total process. Touch, as we have seen, has an immediacy and a credibility unequalled by the other senses and is a primary means of finding out about things among young children as, indeed, in certain contexts – the testing of a knife for sharpness, for example – it is for adults too.

Perhaps the most telling example of this identification by touch of what becomes undeniably real in the world can be found in the Bible when Thomas, later called Doubter, finds that he cannot honestly believe that Jesus has risen from the dead until he has touched the living Christ: 'Then saith he to Thomas, Reach hither thy finger and behold my hands; and reach thither thy hand and thrust it into my side; and be not faithless, but believing.

'And Thomas answered and said unto him My Lord and my God.' (The Gospel according to St John, 20, v 27, 28)

Although the eagerness for tactile involvement diminishes with increasing age and experience, or is to some extent suppressed by the process of socialisation and due regard for convention, even as adults we are not beyond benefit from exploration by touching. Surfaces of many qualities are examined for their texture, particularly those of manufactured or processed materials such as wood, metal and various fabrics. So too do we identify the quality of a person's skin or hair. The 'Wet Paint' sign is as irresistible to some adults as it is to children: how else, after all, can one find out if the paint is still wet or merely new? In such cases the tactile sense gleans more information than can be obtained from vision alone. Nor is the sense of touch entirely lost in celebratory or pleasure-seeking activities: aesthetic interests such as pottery or craft pursuits require an intimacy with the medium which can only be obtained by close contact over a long period. Again, the work of some contemporary sculptors – Barbara Hepworth, for example – occasionally strikes such a commanding balance between the form of the object and the natural form of the material that one is invited to touch in order fully to appreciate the art of the composition.

The work of the creative artist, the musician, the painter, the sculptor, or the sportsman manipulating a ball or a bat, suggests a sensitivity and a coherence in the management of the expressive medium that goes beyond mere instrumentality. There is a kind of physical harmony between the painter and his brush, the potter and his clay or the violinist and his violin such that the exploration of and the insight into the medium is really an advanced form of the child's investigation by touch that we have described earlier. The instrument somehow becomes an extension of the performer's body and the expressive act reflects the individuality of his personality.

Paradoxically, in these examples the expressive acts both transcend the physical contact between the artist and his instrument and yet still depend so vitally upon it. The performance is essentially the communication of an idea, yet the idea has to be projected by means of some form of precise physical control. In this way we speak of the 'touch' of an artist or performer, referring both to his command of the medium and to his formulation of the idea or translation of an emotion. The primary identification in these instances is not, of course of some physical object as was the case in the example of children's play; the artist pursues and identifies a creative concept, an imagined ideal. The work of art, in any medium, is no mere repetition or attempted revival of experience past; it is in a real sense a journey of discovery into new matters and original events.

At a more mundane yet still vitally important level, we use touch to identify and confirm what there is in our various life situations as well as to order, manipulate and control the aspects of our environment that are important to us. Almost every person's day is filled with the touching of literally hundreds or even thousands of objects. Whether we put the kettle on, drive a car, write a letter, do some gardening or simply read, there is a good deal of touching involved. These acts and perceptions of one's own acts of touching are at once outward and positive in their actions on the objects around us and yet inward and receptive in the recognition of the encounter thus made. Touch, in this way, is the ultimate proof of our physical existence, both to ourselves and to others. The world of doing, of constructive or even destructive action, is the reality that is evidence for man's being. Actions are said to speak louder than words and even today, in the highly mechanised age of man substitutes in labouring craftsmanship and thinking, the definitive control of the environment is through this mode. Machines of all kinds have to be handled and manoeuvred: the spade to be grasped, the lathe to be adjusted or programmed, the computer to be instructed by information keyed into a card. It is interesting to note that the second wave of mini-calculators had to be designed to respond more positively in *physical terms* to the operator's touch so that he might be better informed on whether or not he had given the key the right amount of pressure – previously it was possible to duplicate or omit entries unwittingly because of the fine touch required to complete the input circuit.

Thus the proof of our existence in the world may be seen as inherent in the changes we bring about by forceful bodily contact with the object environment. We suggest that this has further important implications. For part, and perhaps the most important part, of these processes lies in the psychological identification of the self. The tactile experience tells us not only of the roughness, the hardness, the resilience, the shape or whatever of the object encountered; it also tells us what *we* are. The very properties exemplified above are not merely (or even necessarily) intrinsic qualities of the object; they are also – and, one might argue, fundamentally – instances of our capacities to sense and understand: it is *we* who experience the situations and subsequently provide the words to explain or describe them. So from very early days we become more aware, more certain, more assured of ourselves by the multiplicity of contacts that occur. We are functionally in the world by these means, and unlike the other senses touch provides a direct and usually irrefutable indication of our being.

To assert that physical contact with the environment is essential for normal development in humans is stating the obvious, yet it is almost impossible to substantiate in those terms since it is unlikely that anyone has grown up entirely without opportunities to make some kind of contact. Various pieces of evidence suggest that this is the case, however, since it has been found that when people are deprived of certain kinds of sensory or perceptual experience they will often suffer some ill effects. In a series of classic experiments carried out at McGill University, subjects were prevented from seeing, hearing or making physical contact with anything except the suit in which they were enveloped. The majority quickly found that this lack of any varied input was quite intolerable* and, although as volunteers they were being well paid to participate, were forced to give up the experiment. Other experiments with young animals, deprived of perceptual learning opportunities at particular stages of their development, showed that they failed to mature normally as we saw from kitten 'roundabout' experiment described earlier in the chapter. Perhaps the most significant evidence for sensory deprivation as the cause of dysfunction is that concerning the effects of maternal deprivation among primates and this we will deal with separately in the next chapter.

Thus, the need to touch and be touched is vital. If the child is somehow prevented from gaining wide tactile experience his capacity for more sophisticated learning is

*John Lilly, in an autobiographical account of similar experiments in which he was the subject, claims the opposite: that such deprivation leads to enhanced self-awareness, meditative states and contact with other psychic forces (*Centre of the Cyclone* Paladin 1973.)

reduced. Such deprivation slows the acquisition of a symbolic framework with which to appraise the world and forces delays on other types of perceptual development. Of special significance in this respect is the touching that occurs in the child's first interpersonal relationships – particularly with his parents. The way in which his mother holds, cuddles and physically cares for him forms a basis for his future relationships and feelings towards the rest of the world.

4 | Social Aspects of Touch

Touching by Others

The act of one person touching another can occur in hundreds of ways and these in turn must subsume a large number of functions. Inter-personal contact will stem from aggression as well as from the desire to care and protect; it may range from friendly competition, through co-operation to self assertive or selfish behaviour; from minor and incidental helping associated with plain good manners or etiquette to the professional services of a manicurist, valet or masseur; and, of course, there is yet another series of functions associated with various forms of sexual contact.

One connotation of touch between two or more people is that it represents the greatest possible amount of closeness. Argyle (1967) has found that the *social* distance between people as perceived, for example, in differences of class, job status or education, is expressed partly by the physical or linear distance between them in the playing out of some social episode. Thus, a worker stands a respectful distance from his boss while lovers may stare into each other's eyes less than a foot apart.

Other factors, such as the direction of looking and the orientation and posture of the body may to some extent modify this finding, as one may observe in a crowded lift or train when strangers often avoid eye contact and attempt not directly to face each other. Unless the situation is a formal one, involving some sort of contact or ritual (as in shaking hands), or is a physical expression of hostility, the

45

closeness of people is broadly indicative of the degree of intimacy, bodily contact representing the most intimate of proximities.

Beyond this, the degree of intimacy implied by touch will depend on the cultural and sub-cultural context and, of course, on which parts of the two bodies are actually in contact. Jourard (1966) has investigated these topics, showing some of the differences that occur with role and sex (Fig. 5) and, typically, the general tendency towards greater amounts of touching between, for example, Latins as opposed to the English.

A second distinction to be made about the touching of others is that it takes place with or without permission. Aggressive and hostile acts such as pushing, jostling, kicking, kneeing, scratching, strangling and so on are patent invasions of the other person's privacy and safety, and, except when performed within a code of rules as in the combat sports of boxing and wrestling, are unwelcome and normally unacceptable without sanction.

When this kind of violence does occur, however, it has its own limiting effects. As Desmond Morris points out (1978), the body-to-body combat of two similarly-equipped species, whether man or tiger, is the safest way of settling disputes, short of acquiescence or the retreat of one party. In unarmed man-to-man combat much physical energy is released, reducing the emotional tension and with it the inclination to continue; further, it is relatively difficult to inflict lethal injury with the body alone; and, above all, the combatants are roughly equal so that the fear of like retaliation to an initially hostile act is always present. The use of weapons such as a pistol with its hidden power removes all these safeguards at a stroke.

We *permit* the touch of another in one of three ways: firstly, through the acceptance of mutually inclusive roles; the health practitioner, the hairdresser or the tailor are paid to attend to our bodies in this way. Secondly, although not entirely distinct from the first, touch is permitted through a personal or individual sanction of the touching activity. Here it matters *who* the person is and whether he is liked, rather than what role he may have.

There is, however, interesting overlap in both of these categories. While we generally feel bound to accept the role-sanctioned touch of the professional (eg. the doctor or the beautician) there are occasions when the personal qualities or attitudes of the particular practitioner make him unacceptable to us so that we are forced to take our request for services elsewhere. Occasionally patients suspect doctors' motives in requiring them to undress or to carry out some kind of physically intimate examination; some people may change their hairdresser because the present one gossips too much – or too little! On the other hand, intimate touch arising from mutual attraction or love of another person also has a role aspect to it. Each of the intimates has, in addition to his *personal* preferences concerning his partner(s), an expectation of the appropriate behaviour for the role of wife, husband, lover, daughter or friend. A wife may expect a supporting arm or a kiss as part of the husband's role. Again, the work of Jourard illustrates this in that there are significant differences in touching behaviour between, for example, friends of the same and of the opposite sex.

A third category of permitted touching is that which is believed to have occurred by accident. In touching, the intention of the initiator is critical because this intention is always explicit and has to be inferred by the recipient of the action. In this case relatively intimate contact is sometimes caused without threat to either party, although one or both may subsequently be embarrassed by it, depending on their ability to reinterpret the situation humorously or otherwise. In this way the short man turning away from the bar and finding himself cheek to breast with a rather taller woman may ignore the contact altogether, apologise profusely, or if he knows the woman, say as a colleague, make some joke about it.

Therefore, it is clear that the amount of physical contact

that is practised in a society is governed by fairly well-defined sets of behavioural norms or unwritten rules which provide both for the individual's role and for the situation he is in at any one time. In our society it is usually accepted that we do not readily or spontaneously give expression to our feelings through the medium of touching someone else, and it will be argued in Chapter 6 that we are generally the poorer for this reluctance.

Be that as it may, a great deal of contact still takes place between people, especially those within the family unit. Here the enormous amount of bodily contact that the mother makes with her baby is of prime importance. In his book *Touching: the Human Significance of the Skin,* Ashley Montague furnishes much evidence to support the idea that such mother (or parent-figure) contact provides security, learning and physical as well as psychological health for the baby. The thesis that a young baby benefits from constant handling or surface contact with its mother is supported by data of two kinds. Firstly, that deprivation causes malfunction, and, secondly, that extra-normal stimulation produces a greater capacity to deal adaptively with the environment.

Where the young are largely or totally deprived of contact there is a high risk of their failing to learn to relate socially to others of the species. Thus, the motherless monkeys of the well-known study by Harlow & Harlow (1962) were socially inactive, very difficult to mate, and (the females), in their turn, were disastrously ineffective as mothers. Montague argues that, in humans, inadequate mother contact may help to cause asthma, dermatitis and other psychosomatic illnesses; it may also contribute to behavioural disorders such as anxiety or schizophrenia. While it remains unlikely that the deprivation of mother touch is a single cause for these ills, the probability of its contribution is not one that can be ignored.

By contrast, it has been shown that when laboratory mammals receive extra handling or gentling they grow larger and heavier than those who do not receive this treatment; moreover, the handled animals are more stable and better able to cope with environmental changes. In cultures where constant mother-child contact is the norm, because the child is carried during the day on the mother's back or side, the children appear to profit from this closeness. Margaret Mead tells of the Balinese children treated in this way: they have a more secure self image, are more sure in their early learning and, as parents, more loving and caring for their own children than their American counterparts.

The literature on early deprivation and stimulation is now extensive, much attention having been drawn to the area by Bowlby (1951). We are concerned with that part of it that considers the effects of human touching and will examine some of the more significant studies in Chapter 7, where they will be seen to relate to the unique potential of man as conceived by the contemporary humanistic approaches to explaining his being and his behaving.

One central function of human touching is that of satisfying sexual needs. In sexual contact touch is both more intimate, in that it extends to parts of the body to which few or no others are allowed access, and more extensive. During intercourse much of each partner's body touches the other's – typically, face, hands chest and abdomen, thighs and, of course, the genital organs which form an erotic focal point, at least for the male. The function of the sexual response, however, must be regarded as complex. Beyond procreation it is another means of self-discovery and self-enhancement; it is erotic and usually pleasure-giving and may be indulged in just for that reason. It is also a social liaison and even in the act of sexual prostitution the exchange has a particular, although different, value for each partner. Sexual intercourse is frequently regarded as the highest and most intense form of expression of love and caring: it is seen as a way of communicating desire, empathy and understanding of one's partner and of indicating acceptance and pleasure of that person in the embrace.

Touch as Communication

As a means of communication, touch is both formal and informal, explicit and implicit; it may be undertaken with care and awareness, or ignorance and indifference, of the feelings of those who make the contact. When we try to define an act of touching as communicative it is always possible that, while such a function exists it, is not the chief concern of the actors. For, as we have already noted, sexual touching has a demonstrating or confiding aspect for many people yet is not, perhaps, generally thought of as an act of communication. Again, a hostile blow has the purpose both of hurting one's adversary and informing him of one's feelings.

Yet there are occasions when touch is predominantly concerned with conveying a meaning between people. Sometimes it means 'I care for you' (arm and hand around the other's shoulders), 'Well done!' (pat on the back or shoulders), 'Watch out', or 'Hold on' (hand grips arm), or 'Look behind you' (tap on the shoulder). In these situations touch is a primary way of communicating; it is more direct, more immediate and is no mere substitute for words; rather is it closer to the original and primitive modes dating back into man's pre-history.

On other occasions, the act of touching may supplement speech, as when a child says 'Go away' and pushes someone from him at the same instant. Similarly, the mother imparts a multiplicity of ideas to her baby by combining voice and body contact: encouragement, restraint, care, joy, playfulness and anger.

In these, as in most communications using touch, there is no unmistakable single meaning: the message, except in some of the most patent expressions of attraction or repulsion cited earlier, is subtly conveyed even within an apparently simple and straightforward contact. In a handshake, for example, much may be implied by the warmth, firmness and duration of the grasp. When the context is familiar and those making the contact understanding of each other communication can be more sophisticated. A kiss is more than just a kiss: it is a lingering, indulgent sharing of closeness; or a mere exchange of formalities; a voluptuous engorging of the other's lips; a dedication, a promise; the hint of seduction in a second's delay; of disinterest in a moment cut short. Shakespeare refers to the exchanges of meaning when Mortimer, unable to communicate with his new Welsh-speaking wife says:

> 'I understand thy kisses and thou mine,
> And that's a feeling disputation.'

'Disputation', here, is used in the old sense of exploring and delineating or thrashing out some scholarly topic, so that the 'feeling disputation' represents a tactile exploration of and coming to terms with the feelings each of the other.

The meaning of various kinds of bodily joinings is some-how founded on the more primitive animalistic behaviours of co-operation, sexual union, play, dominance and defence. The communicative act has, in consequence of this, certain qualities of force or speed that imply the urgency or the delicacy of idea. Three elementary dimensions have been proposed by Rudolph Laban (1974) to describe the quality of any human movement. These are given in Figure 3 as possible categories of tactile movement.

1. FIRM, strong, forceful, using much muscular tension and energy.	FINE TOUCH, delicate, light, with slight tension, buoyant, sensitive.
2. SUDDEN, urgent sharp, instantaneous, of a moment's duration, excited.	SUSTAINED, slow smooth, legato, lingering, prolonged, indulgent of time, unhurried.
3. DIRECT, straight, on a straight line, purposeful, undeviating.	FLEXIBLE, indulgent of space, roundabout, plastic, wavy, generous in attitude toward space.

Fig 3   The three motion factors of weight, time and space as proposed by R Laban (1974)

A touching action may have any combination of qualities

along each of these three dimensions. Where we can identify a touching action as displaying one or more of these motion factors – especially at one extreme of that particular dimension (eg. as strong rather than delicate) – we are thus better informed about the actor's attitude and intentions towards us. For example, the expression of aggression in the form of a push, punch or stab is essentially FIRM and forceful imply- the power of feeling, SUDDEN, stating the immediacy and spontaneity of the response, and DIRECT, showing the un-ambiguous and purposeful intention behind the action. In contrast, in caressing a child's hair or a lover's body one displays the opposing qualities, implying sensitivity, and an indulgence of time and space on the part of the toucher. The reader may consider for himself the corresponding qualities in intention and expression of such acts as shaking hands, tapping on the shoulder, kissing on the lips and soothing the 'bump' on a child's head.

Throughout the discussion of touch as communication, we have made no mention, so far, of the process of communication itself as a complex activity. At this stage it is worth drawing attention to the fact that what at one end of the process is the intention of the actor is by no means necessarily identical or even similar to a message received by any other party. In between these extremes there are points at which the communication may break down or become distorted, as the following diagram (Fig. 4) indicates.

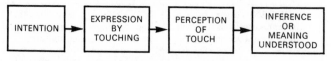

Fig 4　A communication model

When two adults hold hands (usually of opposite sexes in our society, though this may be a normal expression of friendship between two men in some eastern cultures) in walking down the street the initiative in this can sometimes be of importance to both persons concerned. Thus each

might be saying inwardly, after a rather awkward attempt
by A to engage B's hand:

A: 'I can see you want me to be close to you, so I
will hold your hand'

B: 'You are wanting to hold my hand, wanting to be
close to me; therefore I will let you hold my hand'

Here the intention (A wants to please B) and the perception
of this (A wanting to be pleased by B) are quite different.

The difficulty of communication in the light of (often
wrong) assumptions about the other person's frame of
reference is one explored in a penetrating and intelligent
way by Ronald Laing (1970) in his book of poetry, *Knots*.
Communication through touch is no less precarious than
the verbal conversations exploited by Laing: both have their
roots in people's attempts to escape from the essential alone-
ness that is the human condition; both assume that in
making contact the other person's experience is much like
one's own.

When people touch, the action is less likely to be mis-
understood or misconstrued if the episode is formally struc-
tured either by the clearly defined roles of each participant,
ritual, rationalisation or some other statement of intent.
Thus, where the boundaries are drawn and understood,
ambiguity and anxiety are reduced, security is increased and
the touching is fully accepted. The expression of care, concern and gentleness are all implicitly communicated by
nurses in their tactile handling of the patient. In this case
the role of the nurse (giving, caring, tending the body) and
that of the patient (receiving care, accepting treatment) are
known beforehand except by the youngest or the confused
patient.

The Transmission of Spiritual Power
In contrast to more immediate trans-personal acts of communication, touch sometimes forms the basis for the transfer
of power, authority or force of a temporal or spiritual nature.
The farmer's handshake indicates that a deal has been

closed and that the transfer of goods, materials or money will follow. The placing of hands between those of a reigning monarch indicates fealty, implying that all the subject's possessions are at the monarch's disposal. Spiritually, touch channels an awesome transfer of power. The touching of the head in baptism or confirmation by the chosen intermediary between God and Man brings about the transference of the Holy Spirit to that individual. Further from this, touch is used in a more concrete way to harness an external spiritual power in remedy through the medium of the healer. This mode of touch has a long and respected history, stretching from Biblical sources through the treatment of scrofula, a form of tuberculosis, by the monarch's touch, to the present-day spiritualist church. The uses of touch in the healing process form the central theme of this book and will be treated in detail in the next chapter.

Self-Touching
Touching one's own body may not be seen as 'legitimate' in comparison with the functions so far discussed in this chapter all of which have been concerned with the relationship between man and his physical or social environment. It is none the less valid for two reasons: one is that, in touching oneself, one or other of the touching surfaces may be regarded as external in the sense that it is equivalent to an outside stimulus; the other is that in many cases, consciously or otherwise, self-touching may be a substitute for touching by another person. It is also true that self-touching, for whatever reason, is so common that it only becomes noticed when it deviates markedly from the social norm.

There are obvious but important differences between self-touching and that of another. Self-touching does not involve the trespass or violation of another's personal territory or space; no permission needs to be sought nor any granted for an intrusion; there is no anxiety about the motive, effect or acceptability of the touch; and no fear of misrepresentation, misunderstanding or rejection. The touching can be unobtrusive or hidden by other bodily activity so that, at times, even the person himself is unaware that self-touching has occurred.

Self-touching is also a means of exploring and giving pleasure to oneself. Masturbation, a clearly-identifiable example that is seldom openly discussed, has been the subject of a great deal of propaganda, misinformation, taboo and stigma. It provides a relatively straightforward satisfaction to a very basic need, and Desmond Morris (1978) indicates that 'our attitude towards it reflects a more general hostility to the whole business of bodily self-comforting as regressive and narcissistic'.

We serve our bodies in other ways that may be regarded as comparable to the touch of others. In the attempt to comfort or relieve pain after knocking against something hard we rub the injured part; a sore muscle or an aching joint may be massaged to ease the pain. Similar manoeuvres are used to communicate the nature and site of pain to others and Miller (1978) argues that practitioners should pay more attention to these often very accurate non-verbal descriptions of internal abnormalities.

We touch our bodies in many other, less functional ways, in the course of a day, rubbing the jaw, holding the back of the neck, scratching or fingering the nose, supporting the chin on the hands. These actions communicate to others that we are thoughtful, tired, anxious or attentive and it is assumed that such touchings in some way mirror our feelings, although interpretation of such vague and often semiconscious movements is hazardous. Morris (1978) has indicated that these behaviours, which he terms acts of self-intimacy, represent the comfort and relief from stresses and insults of the world that one seeks in the touch of another person. There remains within us as adults the same desire and need for assurance that we experienced as children, but now we have to be content with furtive gratification or the modification of the comforting touch into some socially acceptable form.

5 | The Therapy of Touch

We have up to this point given consideration to physical contact only in its general social context. In this chapter, we intend to look at the more specific occasions where touch takes place within the particular social environment of the health care practitioner. If we consider therapeutic practice in general, we can appreciate that in the relationship between practitioner and client there is the expectation that contact in some form or other will take place, since the practitioner holds a licence, as it were, which allows him access to the client's person without due regard to wider social norms. The client, on the other hand, knows that the practitioner has this licence, sanctions it, and has the expectation that the privilege will be exercised when the occasion merits. Within these socially-defined conditions, touch is often taken for granted and indeed may pass almost unnoticed.

Touch in care practice is used in ways that we first consider as being separate from ordinary social contact. This is not to deny or ignore any overlap between touch in the professional situation and the social patterns with which we are more familiar, since one cannot completely separate the two areas, but we have dealt with it in this way to focus attention on the professional aspects.

Firstly, we can see that touch is used as a therapy in itself, where the contact is channelled into a number of specialised techniques designed to treat and cure somatic ailments that are recognisable through diagnostic labels such as arthritis

57

or muscle strain. Secondly, the medium of touch may be used, often as part of a wider therapeutic programme in an attempt to reach those individuals who appear to be alienated, disturbed or 'marching to a different drum', in order to secure a greater understanding for themselves of their world. Finally, we see in touch, the mode of communication, again within the therapeutic framework, that promotes, establishes and cements a very particular relationship existing between healer and supplicant uniting the intent of both parties. Since this aspect partly overlaps the other two, we will deal with it first.

Touch as a Medium of Communication in Healing

Touching actions are potentially rich as a means of communication. Here, we are concerned with the process and effect of touch in situations where the intention is to restore health. It is more than a logical apposition of these two endeavours – communication and healing – to consider the manner in which bodily contact contains information helpful to a person in need. For many acts of healing necessarily carry communications of one kind or another; and some communications by touch may have a restorative value.

Even when the primary intention of the practitioner is to improve the physical or physiological capacity of the patient his touch must contain other information available to the recipient. The patient understands, from the way he is held, guided, stroked or moved that the practitioner intends a certain kind of physical treatment of his body, whether it is firm or light, rapid or drawn-out, flowing or interrupted. The medium of treatment has its own special message, sometimes clothed, in the patient's view, in the personality traits of the practitioner.

Furthermore, the observant patient attends to and assesses other aspects of the handling of his body: he is able to judge the confidence and competence (and it is not suggested that these qualities necessarily go hand in hand) with which the practitioner performs – a judgement which will materially affect the relationship and subsequent dealings between them, especially in the matters of respect and trust. In the same kind of way the patient may make attributions of 'thoughtful', 'thorough' or 'caring' because he observes the touching to be sensitive to their mutual purpose or quite extensive in its investigative action.

All these communications, however, are secondary to the main intention of the helper, although it is possible that their positive or negative impression on the patient has some impact on treatment outcomes. It will be seen later that communicative touch is used rather more consciously, and even deliberately, in psychotherapy to bring the patient to an increased level of self-awareness in his emotional responses. This is the explicit communication of a particular idea or feeling emanating from the therapist. However, it is not so much the transmission of information that matters here (although progress would be impossible without it) as the *use* of the idea by the patient. His response, ideally, is one which helps him to understand himself better, perhaps to recognise his anxieties or his lack of trust. The recognition is essentially a growth process. It is as though the experience is necessary to compensate for the regression or stunted progress of one who is to some degree alienated from the world of real people and physically-stimulating objects. It is, in this effect, a return to the most basic of all the senses, to the primary nature of experience that we discussed in Chapter 3.

In contrast to these somewhat probing or manipulative processes, touch is also used more empathically to express *caring* attitudes: concern, acceptance, support, protection, respect and love are chief among these. Such expressions are offered from time to time by all the helping professions, although the tendency to adopt a tactile mode for this will vary from one individual to another. To some people, touching is spontaneous and natural in certain circumstances. To others, while the need is recognised, the action of reaching out is laboured and self-conscious; yet others sense no need for touching and, indeed, may find other ways of offering the patient a helpful response.

The kind of communication made by touching depends, again, upon factors other than the act of touching itself. The social and environmental setting of a practitioner-patient interaction affects the interpretation of the contact made. For example, the role and status of the helper – doctor, nurse, teacher, social worker – broadly determines the legitimacy of making contact in showing concern. Privacy or lack of privacy further complicate the meaning of a sympathetic hand on a person's shoulder or a supportive hand in the small of the back. It is also clear that expressive touching is more often initiated by people of higher status – ie. by the practitioner rather than the patient and, between practitioners, more for example by nurses than by aides (Watson 1975). Higher-status helpers are also able to engage in more intimate forms of touching. While the lower arms and back are the commonly used areas of contact to indicate understanding or sympathy, regions closer to the sexual organs – the lower back, the waist and the lower thigh – are touched by those less inhibited by the accepted norms. To some degree all this is confounded by the gender of the two participants. To hold the hand (in comforting) of an opposite-sex patient is somehow more acceptable than treating a same-sex patient in like fashion. Watson has also shown that touching behaviour among female nurses is more frequently directed at mildly rather than severely-impaired patients.

As a form of non-verbal communication, touching may be used to replace rather than supplement the verbal mode. When dealing with the confused elderly patient, or one who has suffered organic brain damage, words are sometimes more of a frustration than a help. Preston (1973) describes a useful regression to the children's world forms of non-verbal communication where the patient is held by the hand to be directed (led) to another part of the room, or grasped by the wrist to indicate that his presence is not wanted where he is.

It is a fine distinction, if any at all, between this attention-drawing use of touch and the business of trying to bring the disorientated patient back to reality. The process of locating the patient in the 'here and now' is sometimes achieved by hand to hand or body contact which in effect says 'Here I am – respond to me'. Such an approach is discussed in more detail later in this chapter in the context of psychotherapy – for the moment an example of the communicative aspect of the type of intervention will suffice.

Preston cites the case of Mr D. who ' . . . can speak, but his remarks centre on his own perceptions, not on those initiated by staff. He is frequently found bending over to pick up articles that only he can see. If a nurse approaches to suggest he take some fluids, he does not react to the request but instead may say,

> "Help me pick these up."
> "Pick them up?"
> "Yes, pick up these boards and hurry."

'But if the nurse puts her hand on his shoulder, he will straighten up and slowly focus his eyes on her. Then if the glass is moved towards his mouth, he will take the glass and drink the fluid willingly. Once his attention is gained, the interaction can be lengthened by taking him, hand-in-hand, and going for a walk where further exchanges can take place.'

Two studies of touch used as a means of communication in the context of nursing care are of sufficient interest and relevance to merit more detailed description. Further, they have taken contrasting and yet complementary approaches to the problems of establishing the effects of touch in the process of care.

Ruth McCorkle, (1974) used an *experimental* research designed in an attempt to *quantify* differences in the effects of touching or not touching on two groups of seriously-ill patients in hospital. The comparison was made with groups controlled for age, sex, and class of patient, as well as for the type of hospital accommodation and care provided. Each patient was approached by the investigator and asked standardised questions about his feelings, and what was happening to him at that time. Recordings of both non-verbal and verbal responses were made using an Interaction Behaviour Worksheet (completed by two independent observers) and an audio-tape of the conversation (later analysed using the Bales' (1970) Analysis).

With those in the experimental group, for the whole of the interaction the investigator, identified by the patients as a nurse, ' . . . touched the patient's wrist gently applying an increase in pressure when asking the three specific questions'. With the control group the investigator did not touch the patients but stood close enough to be touched by them.

Not all the measures revealed differences between the two groups. However, a significantly greater number of these who were touched by the nurse responded with 'positive' facial expressions while a significantly greater number of the control group patients responded with 'negative' facial expressions. Similarly, more of the experimental group reacted positively in what they said to the nurse.

Considering the tightly-controlled and somewhat manipulative nature of this study, it is somewhat surprising that the differences were significant. Touch as a primitive mode of communication is partly subverted by the purpose and conditions of the experiment. What, in the event, was being communicated? Interest, concern or curiosity, perhaps. Nevertheless, this study provides us with evidence, at least in behavioural terms, of the effects of touch in the caring relationship.

More impressive in human terms is the case study reported by Irene Burnside (1973) in which the *quality* of contact in a nursing situation is examined. She tells of her work with six elderly patients, all suffering from chronic brain syndrome. Burnside used touching as the prime means of countering the variety of dysfunctional behaviours caused by this condition, such as babbling, refusal to make eye contact, and social withdrawal. She touched her patients in greetings, helping actions, games and, with three ambulatory men, in dancing. In varying degrees they became more spontaneous and socially aware, sometimes reciprocating the touching gesture.

One cannot do justice to this quite moving account in a few sentences, but the case of Ms. E. is not untypical: 'She kept her eyes closed most of the time, opens them now when I touch her and she is still the most affectionate person in the group . . . She also likes to touch my clothing. I wear wild brightly coloured clothes on group days, often with the tactile quality of cashmere or velveteen. Touching, of course, is a two-way affair – to touch them and let them touch me, my clothing and my jewellery.'

Touch as Physical Therapy

In therapeutic practice, we are able to identify a number of opportunities when contact between practitioner and client may take place. Initially, we will concern ourselves only with those situations where physical contact is used as the instrument of change for the body mechanisms and where the practitioner's intention is to utilise the touch to influence physical systems and thus to alleviate the client's presenting symptoms. It would be difficult within the space of this chapter to describe all treatment procedures where touching is used in this way, or to discuss all the mechanisms through which they act; what we have done, therefore, is to select certain modalities which are representative of the various types of contact. This choice is in no way intended to advertise any particular therapy as being superior, or to comment upon its efficacy; suffice it to say that the therapies concerned have a long history, and have as many adherents as they have critics.

Changes in Anatomical Relationships

Under this heading we can review two distinct areas; orthopaedic surgery, where the changes sought are fairly large ones, and osteopathy, where they are relatively small.

When a joint such as the shoulder has been dislocated as the result of violence, the joint surfaces no longer remain in contact. If there is to be relief of pain and restoration of function, that joint must be reduced, ie. put back into place. To do so, the orthopaedic surgeon will manually restore the surfaces to their proper relationship. In a similar way, after a bone has been fractured it becomes necessary to maneouvre the broken fragments in order to bring them into line as far as possible so that healing can take place with the minimum of deformity. Reduction is carried out partly by sight but principally by feel, although the position of the bones will be confirmed later by radiography. During procedures of this nature, the client will be subjected to a great deal of physical contact, sometimes of an intimate nature such as trespass within the body or handling of the genital region. Furthermore, he may be touched by more than one member of the surgical team in a variety of ways over a considerable span of time. This type of intervention invariably requires the administration of an anaesthetic and, although the client remains unconscious throughout the procedure, we do not know, at the present time, whether there is any form of response to the nature of the interaction. Osteopathy, a profession conceived in 1874 by Andrew Taylor Still but known for hundreds of years before then through the practice of bone setting, will be used to illustrate minor adjustments to the anatomy. Osteopaths would consider that structure and function are two dimensions of the normal organism. When there is a harmonious interplay between these elements, the individual is better able to adjust to and cope with the pressures of everyday life. Abuse, misuse and disuse of the body results in mechanical disturbances that, in some people, lead to . . . 'abnormal reflex patterns which can express themselves in terms of nervous system, neuro-hormonal and neuro-circulatory dysfunctions of various kinds' (Dummer 1978).

These mechanical disturbances give rise to what has been

termed 'osteopathic lesions' which can be thought of as states of stress involving a structure or a function. This state may arise from an obvious external cause such as a strain, a fall, poor posture or infection, or from such factors as anxiety, mental or environmental stresses.

Whatever the cause, however, the client is left with some impairment of body function which, if allowed to remain, will result in tissue change. The osteopath attempts to restore the skeletal structures to their proper order by . . . 'expert and controlled movements of the skeletal structure to restore mobility and to "straighten out the kinks" ' (Scott). This allows the body to make full use of its own self-regulating abilities. From the literature available (Hoag *et al* 1969; Stoddard 1977) it can be seen that the various maneouvres do produce changes in both signs and symptoms, but Dr John Lester (Eagle 1976) has put forward the challenging idea that a proportion of the benefits gained from osteopathy come not from the anatomical changes but rather from other healing abilities of the practitioner.

Changes in Physiological Systems

Under this heading we will consider massage, the Anatriptic Art, one of the most ancient of the therapies known to mankind. We should remind ourselves that almost any movement of the hands over the body can and has been said to constitute massage of some sort and so we might consider actions such as the gentle rubbing and patting of a baby's back by the mother to induce tranquillity and sleep; or the more esoteric ministrations used in Eastern sexual practices. The art has been practised by professional therapists, yogi, parents, friends, lovers and ladies of dubious reputation, for reasons ranging from sexual enlightenment, physical and psycho-therapy, pleasure and, of course, financial profit. Massage, because of the uses to which it has been put throughout history, has suffered, like Hamlet, from the slings and arrows of outrageous fortune; we shall not get too involved in the non-medical aspects but confine our-

selves to massage as defined by Beard & Wood (1964) as
' . . . the term used to designate certain manipulations of
the soft tissues of the body; these manipulations are most
effectively performed with the hands, and are administered
for the purpose of producing effects *on the nervous and
muscular systems and the local and general circulation of the
blood and lymph* (present authors' italics).

Techniques

There are as many ways of performing massage as there are
practitioners, because each person will adapt, convert or
invent manoeuvres according to his abilities, needs and per-
suasions. Although various texts appear to show a vast number of techniques we can describe them under five basic
headings.

Stroking (Effleurage)   The hand or hands of the practitioner are placed palm downwards on the client's body: the
hands then move over the part while full contact is retained,
moulding themselves to the anatomical contours, the pressure varying from a very light caress to a firm deep stroke.
The direction may run along the line of the veins, that is
towards the heart, or it may be in the opposite direction,
while in some instances the stroking may be in a circular or
random manner.

Kneading (Petrissage)   The tissues are grasped and released in one or both hands, either together or alternately in
lifting, kneading, wringing or pressing movements.

Percussion (Tapotement)   Performed as a brisk succession
of controlled hitting movements of the hands used alternately. The little finger border is used (hacking) the cupped
hands (clapping) or the half-closed fist (beating). As with
stroking the contact may be light or heavy. These three
categories contain the majority of massage strokes used
today.

Vibration   This is a shuddering or shaking movement of the
practitioner's hands in contact with the client. It is sometimes used for gaining relaxation but is more often found in

physiotherapeutic techniques of clearing sputum from the chest after surgery. Vibrations may be fine or coarse.

Friction A deep rotary or transverse pressure with the thumb or fingers given over a localised area of the body, such as a ligament or a tendon, normally used only by physiotherapists to produce a traumatic hyperaemia and movement of the structure concerned (Cyriax 1971).

Physiological Effects of Massage

If stroking or kneading movements are made in the direction of the venous return to the heart, the blood present in the vessels will be forced forwards rather like toothpaste in a tube. This leaves a space, as it were, for more blood to enter and take its place. The stimulation of the sympathetic nervous system by the massage creates a dilation of the tiny superficial vessels which is seen as a reddening of the skin. This reaction, plus the mechanical squeezing, contribute to a state in which tissue circulation and exchange is facilitated, waste products are removed and nutrition of the tissues is improved.

The lymphatic system is a complex intercommunicating network of small vessels which act as an extra drainage channel for fluid that has seeped out of the blood vessels, as well as providing many of the cell elements for the counteraction of infection. Movement of fluid within these vessels is dependent on forces outside the system such as gravity and muscle activity. Massage, particularly if the arm or leg is placed higher than the heart, makes use of these two external forces and can make an important contribution to the treatment of chronic inflammatory conditions where the free movement of lymph and tissue fluid is prevented (Drinker & Yoffey 1941).

It is claimed that massage has a beneficial effect on the metabolism of the skin but this may in part be due to the circulatory effects mentioned above.

It has been stated by Pemberton (1950) that massage produces an increase in the number of red cells in the circulating blood, as well as a rise in haemoglobin, and also that there is a small but measureable increase in the oxygen-carrying capacity of the cells.

Barr & Taslitz (1970) undertook a study of the effects of back massage on the autonomic nervous system. They measured arterial blood pressure, heart rate, respiration rate, galvanic skin response, skin temperature, body temperature and pupil diameter in ten subjects before and after massage, and found an increase in the activity of the sympathetic nerves in most of the indexes.

Energy Transference
We are concerned here with that phenomenon which can be termed the laying on of hands, a tradition going back at least as far as biblical times; St Luke, himself a physician, describes how Jesus by his touch cured an old woman who had been crippled for eighteen years (St Luke 13:13). The practice of the laying-on of hands as a therapy indicates that the healer places his hands on the sick person and that person becomes well. Many practitioners of this form of therapy consider that they have no special power in themselves but that they are mere agents through whom the healing process is activated. Some claim to know the source of that power but others remain bewildered by it. These power sources appear to emanate from

1   the good offices of disembodied spirits: these may be of individuals who once lived on this earth, some of them famous physicians, others as people unknown to us now, or they may be as formless and nameless inhabitants of a supernatural world;
2   a supreme Deity; the God of our Christian tradition;
3   the sick person himself, the healer mobilising what Hippocrates called the *Medicatrix Naturae Vitae*, that is, the body's natural recuperative powers; or
4   the actual interaction between healer and client resulting in the transference of 'energy' from one to another.

Few opportunities have arisen to subject the claims of practitioners to scientific scrutiny. We would argue that anecdotal evidence is not necessarily invalid but we would prefer to concentrate on those aspects that do have some experimental proof.

Grad (1961; 1964) conducted experiments, using mice and, later, barley seeds, in which he attempted to quantify the effects of a well-known healer called Oskar Esterbany. In one series, 300 mice were given similar back wounds: 100 of these animals, enclosed in containers, were held in Esterbany's hands twice a day for a quarter of an hour for five-and-one-half days per week; a further 100 were treated by being held by people with no known healing ability, and the last 100 were left untreated. After a fortnight the mice who had been held by Esterbany showed a greater amount of wound healing.

Grad also used barley seeds which had been soaked in saline. Some of these were watered with ordinary tap water, others with water from beakers that had been held by Esterbany and the remainder with water from beakers held by 'non-healers'. The seedlings from the Esterbany group sprouted more quickly, grew taller and had more chlorophyll than did the others.

In the 1970s Krieger (1972; 1975) began research using human subjects and attempted to demonstrate that there would be a measurable change in some of the body elements after treatment by a healer. She set out to test the hypothesis that, under experimental conditions in two groups of people with no significant difference in haemoglobin levels, there ought to be a difference in these levels between those who were treated by a recognised healer and those who were not.

The results indicated that this was the case and that after healing sessions involving the laying on of hands there was a rise in haemoglobin levels.

We have seen that to justify the practice of osteopathy we can put forward a theory which fits into our knowledge of the disease process: it is true that this theory has not received total approval by all shades of medical opinion but, nevertheless, it is plausible. Massage is perhaps more obviously part of what we know about the physiology of the human body. The laying-on of hands took us a little further from what we might term conventional practice but, even so, the underlying pathological processes remained familiar.

Our fourth example, however, will move us not only further from familiar practice but will involve us in a whole new theoretical concept based on the oriental, mainly Chinese, philosophy of ill health. Acupressure, G-Jo and Shiat-su are all various terms used to describe therapies in which finger or thumb pressures only are used on specific sites on the body, to prevent and to cure illness. To understand why by simply pressing on the skin the practitioner can do this, we need to consider a brief outline of the philosophy underlying this therapy. First of all, let us say that this is no obscure Johnny-come-lately idea, the first text appearing about 4000 years ago as *The Yellow Emperor's Classic of Internal Medicine*, a work which should still be of interest to those concerned with a holistic approach to care.

The ancient Chinese did not consider the body to be set apart from the external world, but, rather that it formed a part of it, participating in an interaction that is eternally changing. Pervading every part of the universe is the energy called Ch'i, the essential stuff of life itself: this energy is influenced by the two principles Yin the negative and Yan the positive, and everything that exists does so as the interplay between these principles.

Man is involved with two environments, the external one which includes such things as work, the country that he lives in, the climate, etc, and an internal one, of his cellular activity, emotional state and the condition of the Ch'i. Health is the perfect harmony between these two environments, separated as they are by the skin and dependent on the exact balance of Yin and Yang thus ensuring an harmonious distribution of Ch'i throughout. Ch'i is said to flow through the body along fixed pathways called meridians; along these meridians lie points (acupoints) which seem to act as signal boxes controlling and regulating the energy flow so that it is even, and preventing a situation where there is an excess or a deficiency of Ch'i to any part of the body. Occasionally, the body's internal environment becomes 'out-of-tune' with the external, causing a disturbance in energy flow. Normally, the acupoints adjust the flow as part of the body's natural ability to regulate and heal itself. If they are unable to do so then the disturbed flow will affect the whole body resulting in symptoms of some sort and what we would call illness. It becomes the intent of the practitioner to influence the acupoints in such a way as to redistribute the flow.

Treating ill health then requires two factors:

1   correction of the environmental balance by diet, exercise or a change in life style; and
2   adjustments, via the acupoints, of the energy flow sedating some, toning up others, using needles (accupuncture), heat (moxibustion), or pressure (acupressure).

Traditional western examination and diagnosis is inappropriate in this philosophy of health care and the features of the eastern way of assessing health would seem alien to our thinking. A description of this is irrelevant to our text but interested readers are referred to Felix Mann's book (1972).

Techniques of Acupressure
Firm and deep pressure is given with the tip of the finger or thumb held at right angles to the skin. Stimulation may be given by moving the finger in a clockwise or anti-clockwise direction for a period ranging from half a minute to three or four. If the acupoint is represented on both sides of the body then both may be treated. It is important to select the appropriate point and then to treat it for the shortest time necessary: twice the time does not give twice the effect. The

practitioner's mind must be focused on the task and Lawson Wood (1978) states that he should fix in his mind the result that he wants as if that result had already been achieved.

We have tried to show some therapies in which the contact is used to produce changes in the client's body and in the following chapter we will be looking at ways in which the practitioner attempts to reach non-physical functions of the client. In doing so we have appeared to subscribe to traditional western medical philosophy in that we have separated physical and non-physical elements rather than treating them as integral pairings.

This dualism has led us to the situation where we have on the one side, practitioners whose thinking is dominated by the physical findings and measurements, and who pays only lip service to the client's emotions, feelings and fears. On the other side, we have practitioners who consider ill health to be largely the product of events stored up, hidden and repressed over a lifetime. The Chinese philosopher would see the individual as a whole person in whom it would be impossible to separate physical from mental since external manifestations are ' . . . but two inseparable expressions of what is unalterably one' (Mann 1972).

We would argue that touch is a medium through which we can lower the rather false boundaries between these two elements and we would agree with the idea that they are merely shadows thrown by the same object.

6 | The Use of Touch in Psychotherapy

Mental Illness as Socially Caused

To be labelled as mentally ill still attaches to one a degree of stigma, especially when it is generally known that an individual has been referred for treatment (which we call *psychotherapy* to include all forms of such treatment) and is obliged to stay in hospital for a period of time. His subsequent behaviour is much more likely to be interpreted in the light of his previously-labelled condition: his unusually quiet or excessively demonstrative behaviour – his anger, for example – are accounted for by his defined condition *even when he has recovered from it*, more than by a normal reaction to the demanding environment with which we all struggle for an existence. For a full and interesting account of this phenomenon see Irving Goffman's book *Stigma: Notes on a Spoiled Identity*.

Mental illness, therefore, has aspects that strongly depend on the conceptions and attitudes of others, especially those to whom the patient is well-known. In the early stages of some psychological abnormality it is often the sufferer's friends or relatives, distressed by his behaviour, who arrange for professional intervention, sometimes in conflict with the patient's own desires. In this respect mental illness may be regarded as social non-conformity and any action taken attempts to deal with the problems created by the illness for others as it attempts also to work for the patient's individual benefit.

The difficulties of identifying cause in mental illness are

added to by an historic, and perhaps unjustifiable, tendency to comparison with physical illnesses. Thus, a medical model of illness makes two primary assumptions: one, that the condition has one or more antecedent causes in the physical or chemical functioning of bodily processes, and the other, that it is this condition that makes a person ill – ie. that the absence of such a state enables us to declare that person well again. However, in mental illness either or both of these assumptions may be inappropriate – the condition may not be accounted for in physical or medical terms. Indeed many existentially-orientated therapists (see, for example, Laing, 1959) would say that the problem, its cause and its solution are definable only in terms of the patient's experience. In other words, the strange and socially dysfunctional behaviour of the mentally ill is to be regarded as no more than that from the outsider's point of view. It may be odd but it does not necessarily arise from something foreign or alien inside the body. Thus a mental illness is seen as a way of behaving that depends upon previous and present experience and is logically and sensibly related to that experience. The abnormal behaviour is not so when seen in this relationship. It is essentially 'normal' when seen in relation to the development and evolution of the individual personality. In this sense it is not an illness and certainly is not comparable to medical illnesses such as influenza or cancer, for the cause is not apparently related to the presence of hostile micro-organisms or physical malfunction.

Thus, we have the position that mental illness is a socially-deviant condition usually involving an emotional imbalance which relates, although not always consciously, to the previous experience and perhaps the present circumstances of the patient. This past experience, of course, is usually chiefly concerned with the relationships with others, particularly, as Laing argues, with members of the family in the patient's childhood. Because of the social origins and implications of mental illness, its treatment whether in the clinic, the hospital or the community must consider the patient's relationships with others, especially the psychotherapist. It is the way in which the therapist relates, the rationale behind his approach to the patient is the most important part of the effort to help. In this therapists differ. Traditional psycho-analysis offers a personally-detached and clinically-interpretative style, while the client-centred approach of Carl Rogers specifies particular attitudes important for the success of therapy and explicitly avoids interpretation of the client's story. The conscious and deliberate use of touch in this relationship, therefore, is of concern to all involved in such a transaction. It is clearly a potent social act in what we have taken some pains to describe as a socially-skilled treatment of a socially-caused and manifested problem. Whether it can be employed to the benefit of the patient requires more than a generalised answer and we shall investigate this in the next section.

Whatever effect bodily contact may have in the therapeutic relationship it is worth noting here that it is not limited to that context alone. Mental illness, as we have seen, is not simply something that you have or haven't 'got'; it is not an all-or-none phenomenon. If, as we have argued, it is wholly or mainly caused by social events we are all more or less susceptible to these and to consequent loss of health. That this is the case is illustrated by our reaction to the various stresses and crises of life, which may make us anxious, depressed, confused, helpless, unable to sleep or work, and so on. These are symptoms which differ only in degree and persistence from those of patients committed for psychotherapy. Even on a more mundane basis one may be sufficiently self-aware to notice one's own reaction on not being noticed by somebody who is expected to offer a greeting. The interpretation of this situation as a deliberate snub, a temporary indifference or a preoccupation with something else is as much a reflection of one's own state of health as it is any intention or lack of intention on the part of the other person. The same kind of prejudice may also exist in competitive settings where suspicions of a rival sometimes reflect more of paranoia in one participant than of dishonesty in another. What we have to say about the effects of touch in the more formal therapeutic location will also apply to some degree in other contexts, especially, of course, those featuring a helping relationship.

Mental Illness & Touch

How far, then, can bodily contact with another assist that person in a healing or therapeutic way? Common sense and observation of everyday events would suggest that touch used in an appropriate manner has a therapeutic value for many if not for all of us. The older person who has lost his spouse finds the touch of a friend or a caring relative to be a comfort especially when he is feeling lonely or uncared for. The toddler runs to his mother when a stranger approaches him or some new turn of events threatens his security: he clings closely to her and is happier when she cuddles him in return.

The infant who is uncared for at home seems constantly to seek attention in school, touching or holding the hand of any adult who happens to come into the classroom. Sometimes such an infant will seek contact by climbing on to the lap of or clinging to a complete stranger. Cynthia Kee (1980) describes a project in which the teacher's commitment to holding and cuddling proved successful in helping preschool problem children.

A few children may be so desperately in need of contact that they negotiate for physical punishment as a substitute for touching or attention of a more amicable kind. Such behaviour may relate to a later tendency towards masochism where pain, normally to be avoided, becomes a form of pleasure required to satisfy the desire for a physically-close relationship which the person cannot obtain in other ways. The pain experienced is felt as exquisite and helps to establish the reality of the relationship and of himself.

Touching the client or allowing the client to touch the

therapist is more consciously controlled since it is part of a professional's actions in therapy and may, of course, have important political, legal and moral implications as well as those directly concerned with therapy. It has therefore been discussed, though not extensively so, in books and professional journals. Most sources seem to agree on a number of aspects of bodily contact which help the patient towards an understanding of the problem and provide some support in dealing with it.

As indicated above (in the case of masochism), touch provides confirmation of being in the world for some individuals who are in special need of this – proof of the reality of themselves and others. Touch is an indication of acceptance; it tells the patient that his helper has a continuing commitment to him as a person; that he understands, empathises and is willing to go on with the therapy even though the patient is anxious, rejecting, aggressive or doubtful either in relation to himself or to the therapist. Because touch is an act of intimacy it may, in the right circumstances, assist the client in the process of bringing up and discussing deeper and more intimate aspects of the problem – aspects which he himself is hardly aware of. The more intimate forms of touching usefully extend, in the opinion of some therapists, to explicitly sexual behaviour and to symbolic mothering. It is argued that this kind of physical contact in an appropriate context will develop some awareness in the client of the roots of his problem. As might be anticipated none of these proposed benefits are unqualified or without some risks. The following sections, therefore, discuss in rather more detail their nature and application.

Orientating to Reality

It is perhaps difficult for many people who are very much involved in practical activities of all kinds – running a home, servicing a car, or manufacturing and selling goods – to understand the doubts and anxieties that some patients have about themselves and about the extent to which they are 'real' or are positive agents in the world* Even among the healthy, a person's self-assurance may be disturbed and his sense of reality distorted as the experiments of Asch (1956), previously described, have shown (p. 24). The fact that six or seven people of 10 are somehow persuaded to make a false judgement on this visually straightforward line-comparison task is less important for us here than the great sense of self doubt, loss of assurance, extreme dismay and anxiety that *all* of the bone fide subjects in the experiment seemed to experience at the time and were able to report afterwards. In these exceptional circumstances most people would reveal a need for reassurance until they can satisfactorily explain to themselves what is happening.

It is by means of touch that some mentally ill patients re-establish their sense of being in the world. We referred in Chapter 3 to the primary nature of touch as a sensory experience, showing that it is with this sense that a young baby learns discriminate himself and his environment. Using the tactile sense puts us most 'in the world'. Burton & Heller (1964) point out that, as cultures evolve, the sensory qualities of immediate experience tend to be relinquished for intellectual forms more conceptual in nature; our worlds are becoming symbolic; we deal with ideas more than practicalities; our jobs increasingly are about figures and words, communication and mental conflict; only rarely do they demand physical as well as intellectual skill. Thus, there may be in the individual a progressive estrangement and alienation from his body. Man is less in touch with his body today than he has been at other periods in history. The ancient Greeks, for example, idealised the human form as representative of man's prowess and completeness in many and varied spheres of activity. Since the philosophical ideas of Descartes

*For a readable account giving insight to the inner life of a young schizophrenic girl, the reader is referred to *I Never Promised You a Rose Garden* by Hannah Green, first published in 1964 by Victor Gollancz Ltd.

in the first half of the 17th century the image of man as a mind-body dichotomy has contributed towards an increasing tendency to invest remedial measures in medicine mostly in the physical or bodily dimension, failing in the process to recognise the essential *inter*dependence of these two conceptual aspects of man's being. Drugs are used to alleviate anxiety – physical palliatives for a mind-body malaise. Indeed, the idea of a whole-person approach to an intervention whether it is medical, social or educational is really only just beginning again to permeate the helping professions.

Ironically, Sigmund Freud, among the first to recognise and treat mental illness as having psychological rather than purely physical origins, and who began by using touch to establish a good psychotherapeutic relationship, soon found the prevailing prudish Victorian attitudes prevented his continuing with this practice.

The use of touch in psychotherapy goes some way towards restoring the harmony of mind and body enabling the patient to come to terms simultaneously with his own beliefs and the attitudes, expressed through contact, of another person. Mintz (1969) describes the case of a woman who as a child had almost been strangled by her mother. Haunted by fears and images of being strangled she was yet unable to connect these with her childhood experience. She spoke of a recent dream on this subject without any apparent feeling of being strangled. On some pretext the therapist crossed behind the patient's chair and put her hands lightly around the woman's throat. The patient screamed, the therapist released her immediately and stood by her chair holding her hand. The woman experienced great relief and subsequently was more sharply aware that her strangling episode was in the past. Mintz explains the effect of the touching as enabling the fantasy to become real and be dealt with on a realistic level.

More commonly in general nursing and other caring situations – mothering for example – touch is used in the face of illness, fear or anxiety to provide the reassurance that someone else is available and will help. One significant aspect of this is to re-establish and maintain sufficient awareness in the stressed person for him to cope adequately with the demands of situation. The child waking from a nightmare sometimes has difficulty in releasing himself from the dream experience. His mother or father can help this by providing physical contact, which helps to locate him in the 'here-and-now', as well as conveying care and love. Hospital patients recovering from critical phases of their illnesses tell of the importance of a nurse or relation in making some kind of demand of them to regain their health, forcefully communicated by the use of touch implying the urgency and desperation felt by the carer. In this context, touch provides a strongly-motivating power to respond to what is happening 'out there' in the world. Touch has dynamic qualities – changes of temperature, pressure, texture and of physical location on the body; it adds up to the presence of another human being; it signals his *enduring* attitudes as well as a variety of changing states within those; it *demands* attention of all but the weakest, apathetic or most asocial of persons. To respond to this demand, to follow these meanings and variations in meaning moves the patient towards a state of being more fully in the world.

Touch as Acceptance

A second value of touch in therapy is to communicate a sense of acceptance to the client or patient. Many patients, for various reasons, have strong feelings of self-disapproval amounting in some cases to a disgust with or loathing of the self. This may be connected with a physical defect or disability, early family experience perhaps involving parental disapproval or disappointment, or the shame felt because of sexual promiscuity or deviance. Mintz, for example, mentions the case of a young married textile designer who had previously spent some months as a call girl. She displayed 'an intensely masochistic shame . . . and found these memories extremely painful. Without thinking it through I found that as I escorted her to the door after each session I would usually lay my hand lightly on her shoulder. It is my opinion that without this symbol of acceptance she would have been too overwhelmed by shame and embarrassment to remain in treatment'.

In psychotherapy and, indeed, in counselling (which in the most widely used form developed by Carl Rogers uses the same techniques as psychotherapy*) there is frequently a time during the interview when the client's emotional reaction to the subject he is bringing forward is intense. He may respond by letting his anger, grief or even joy overflow in a total bodily expression of his feelings. This process of catharsis is of benefit to the client and generally to be encouraged. It is, however, not within the prevailing norm for public behaviour and is therefore carefully restrained by most of us. To assist the client in catharsis the therapist 'gives permission' by reaching out to him and placing a hand on his hand, arm or shoulder. In a society where it is not acceptable for men to cry this non-verbal signal of acceptance and empathy to the client who is in tears facilitates the release and encourages its progress to a natural conclusion. In this kind of encounter the patient is again receiving reassurance in the emotional journey into himself. The freedom to explore and accept one's emotions, so vital in becoming aware and free from unconscious controls of action is not easily obtained for oneself, partly, as we have seen because of strong social influences and partly because this new territory for most of us is disturbing or even frightening in prospect. Touch can help to counterbalance this effect by saying to the client 'You are here (because you can feel me). I am here with you to support and help.'

In another form of counselling activity known as peer or

*See Rogers C. R. (1961) *On Becoming a Person: A Therapist's View of Psychotherapy.* Houghton Mifflin. Some people argue (Rowan 1976) that psychotherapy and counselling are the same process. Be that as it may, the counsellor usually meets people whose problems have not so far led them to a state of diagnosed illness.

co-counselling touch is more deliberately employed. In this each participant takes the role of counsellor and client in turn; the available time is shared between the two according to some pre-arranged contract. Some previous training and experience is needed for *both* roles, however, so that the session is of maximum benefit to the two persons. One bodily position frequently adopted by the co-counsellors is sitting cross-legged on the floor facing each other and holding both hands. Again, this serves to maintain the client in the 'here-and-now' when this is needed and to provide tangible evidence of support and sympathy.

Touch and Self-disclosure

One might have assumed that the process of making the self known to another – self-disclosure – was facilitated by the intimacy of contact with that person. Much depends, of course, on how any particular instance of touching is employed in the context of therapy – whether, for example, it is used with advance warning and explanation in a formal and explicit manner (as one kind of extreme) or whether its meaning is implicit or assumed by the therapist and its use appears casual or incidental. Apart from these obvious difficulties of interpretation there is still scant evidence to suggest that touching the patient actually helps him to 'open up' with his problems.

Jourard's (1966) original and now quite famous study of body accessibility established that the highest rates of tactile exchange occurs between close friends of the opposite sex: the implication here is that touching and intimacy generally are closely related. However, a later study (Jourard & Rubin 1968) failed to demonstrate any correlation between the two modes of self-disclosure and touching. It has been proposed that differences between cultures account for these findings, and, in a later investigation with 190 Israeli students, Lomranz & Shapira (1974) reported a strong positive correlation between self-disclosure and touching, particularly between close friends of the same or the opposite sex. The

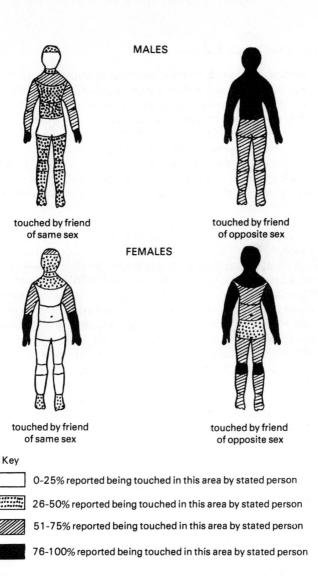

MALES

FEMALES

touched by friend
of same sex

touched by friend
of opposite sex

touched by friend
of same sex

touched by friend
of opposite sex

Key

0-25% reported being touched in this area by stated person

26-50% reported being touched in this area by stated person

51-75% reported being touched in this area by stated person

76-100% reported being touched in this area by stated person

Fig 5 S M Jourard's study on Body-accessibility shows the extent
to which 308 unmarried American college students reported being
touched by friends of the same and opposite sexes

conclusions from this research are not necessarily applicable to the quite different relationship established between patient and therapist. At best it might be urged that where the therapist is perceived as a friend as well as a professional helper self-disclosure is assisted by the act of touching.

There are several factors that may confuse the issue, however. While, in general, touch may be seen as permitted within the helping role of the therapist, it may also be seen as demonstrative of his superior status in the relationship. Observational studies by Henly (1973) show that touch privilege is a correlate of status. Such an effect would serve to *distance* rather than closen the attitudes of the participants.

The act of touching is frequently construed as having sexual connotations. Jourard & Rubin (1968), for example, take the view that 'touching is equated with sexual intent either consciously or at a less conscious level'. Again, with a better knowledge of any individual within a given culture or a specified professional situation touching may simply be accepted as a part of the therapist's personality. 'Some people touch a lot; others don't' is a typical attribution of this kind.

It would appear that, short of some carefully prepared transaction in which client and therapist shared expectations about the usefulness of body contact as an aid to self-disclosure, little is actually to be gained by touching on the therapist's part. The area has not been much investigated, however, and in any case is bound to be affected by the prevailing culture and sub-culture and the changes that occur in these.

The Use of Touch in Transference
Transference in psychotherapy is one of the fundamental processes of adaptive change in the patient. Its effect depends upon the assumption that earlier relationships in the patient's life are the source of intense but conflicting emotion; that although these lie buried in the patient's unconscious

mind (ie. he is unable to remember them) they are nonetheless preventing him from functioning adequately and without undue strain in day to day life. Transference occurs at the stage of recovery when these feelings are just coming into the patient's awareness. Lacking any real understanding of their origin but disturbed by their intensity he rationalises them as due to the therapist. During the course of treatment he may thus feel love and hatred, dependence and aggression, fear and security that he has experienced but never fully acknowledged with others, especially the parents, friends, lovers, heroes and oppressors of his early childhood. All of these are experienced towards the therapist, who uses the transference relationship to help the patient to acquire insight into his own personality and to understand the implications of these emotions.

Touch in this or any other helping context is not, of itself, a panacea. Its effectiveness in facilitating transference and enabling personality growth to take place depends on the attitude and motivation of the two parties concerned. Spotnitz (1971) distinguishes between mere gratification bodily contact which ' . . . smothers the incentive for change and fixates the patient at his current level of development and touching which assists maturation'. The latter, he argues, is governed by a therapeutic contract so that when touching occurs (in group psychotherapy) it is examined in relation to group rules, explicitly or implicitly established, to see whether it has a constructive or destructive effect on the proceedings. Touching apparently is grist to the verbal mill which, for Spotnitz, represents the main if not the only method of gaining understanding.

This rather deliberate approach contrasts with others which view freer and more natural uses of bodily contact as prime aspects of being oneself as fully and honestly as possible. While the effects of this are also open to discussion, communication takes place at non-verbal levels, sometimes in more primitive but also in more direct and powerful ways. Patient awareness is stimulated by the implicit openness and spontaneity in the person-to-person encounter, encouraging and freeing him to attend to his own responses to what is going on.

The possibility of the therapeutic contract extending to include full sexual intercourse is advocated by some who claim that it enables the therapist to obtain a fuller understanding of the client's sexual problems, provides the patient with a sexual partner who is free from guilt and fear and allows him to explore his emotions in the safe relationship of the transference. Given that such physical intimacy is no mere self-indulgence for either party (and the dangers of this are obviously great where there is a degree of physical compatibility and sexual interest – how else could it occur? – between the patient and therapist) it appears to be a logical progression of the uses of bodily contact already proposed.

Mintz, however, puts a cogent case against this. She argues that although the therapist may be able to maintain complete objectivity, ' . . . this very objectivity must necessarily create a situation in which sexual experience would become mechanical and lacking in emotional value. Control and condescension rather than mutuality would mark the relationship'. Even allowing for the greater sexual freedom and tolerance that our society shows at present, it is difficult to see how the risks inherent in maintaining a sexual relationship in therapy and the possibility of damage to both patient and therapist could be worth the possible therapeutic gains.

Conclusions

The act of touching another person who needs some sort of help with problems of coping with his life is not, of itself necessarily helpful; it may, as we have shown, be detrimental to the patient. Obviously, touching in general must include acts of aggression and hostility as well as of kindness and love. We are quick to protect our patient from physical injury or threat; psychological damage, although harder to detect, perhaps, is no less important. With rare exceptions when the therapist has a special understanding of the patient it is better not to risk the obvious hazards of aggressive or overtly sexual contact.

On the other hand there are many instances where touch as we have seen can provide support, reassurance and orientation just as it can reinforce a helping relationship. The norms of British society operate against touching behaviours when they are to be used as expressions of loving and caring. This helps to prevent bodily contact in settings where the practitioner, with sufficient knowledge of himself and his patient, might otherwise have used it to good effect. Generally, we could profitably explore the use of bodily touching in therapy more than we do at present.

7 | Touch and the Humanistic Experience

We have so far considered the beneficial effects of touch within the more-or-less controlled settings of medical treatment and therapy. The expectations of both patient and practitioner of what is right and proper in this relationship largely determine the extent to which either party is free to initiate touching of the other. Most, if not all of the touching that does occur relates to the 'helping' or curative role played by the health agent. Because our view of the healing process is that it is to be observed and assisted by means of scientific principles, most of the restorative process of touching will be justified in mechanistic terms invoking the need for access and control, safety and support. Less emphasis is given to the psychological effects of touching and being touched, perhaps because these are more difficult to control and measure, probably because, except for the 'medical' touching the outside norms of social behaviour would apply and almost certainly because neither party can see a need for it. Attempts at making contact to improve patient morale or to create a feeling of well-being are seldom made except where a group of patients have a clear need as, for example, in work with children or the elderly.

Humanistic Groups

By contrast to these rather conservative attitudes there exists amongst a number of voluntary and self-help groups a rather more permissive use of touch in the caring process. These groups are consciously aiming to use the experience of touch as a means of developing awareness of oneself, of submerged feelings; also of the joyful* and celebratory nature of the shared experience. These groups exist under the umbrella of humanistic or person-centred psychology, an approach which affirms the importance and validity of a person's *experience* in contrast with what others, even experts, may construe about his behaviour; such groups may also be called 'growth' or 'encounter' groups. Many of them use bodily contact as a means of learning and understanding and some are predominantly concerned with this experience, Chief among these are Reichian therapy, Rolfing groups (following the principles of Ida Rolf) or, more recently, the Sensory Awakening groups of Bernard Gunther. Such activities and others like them may be called bio-energetics, massage or simply bodywork. Most of this chapter will be spent in discussion of the methods and functioning of these bodywork groups.

Two assumptions are common amongst humanistic groups. One is that the individual has suffered (as well as benefited) from experiences with others, especially early in life, and that these hinder and even prevent him from functioning properly and living fully; to some extent most of us are maladjusted and need some help to achieve what we are capable of and want to do. The other assumption, a more positive expression of the same idea, is that each person has a unique potential for growth and that, ideally, his experiences and encounters with the world will provide exactly the right amount of challenge or demand, of variety and satisfaction, to allow the process of unfolding and learning to continue. Growth groups are fundamentally directed at these two aspects of experience, although different disciplines employ different group structures and techniques; most, however, establish a caring atmosphere where touch is used more

---

*'Joyful' may seem to be an exaggerated claim in this context; the reader is referred to William Schutz (1967) in his description of encounter groups: *Joy*, Penguin Books.

freely than is normal in other comparable mutual interest groups. For example, in some groups the usual form of greeting – a hello or a handshake – is replaced by a full bodily embrace or hug. Again, when the unity of a group is expressed or the group as a whole attends to its shared interest, people stand in a circle close enough for their bodies to touch, with arms around each others' shoulders or trunks.

Some of the work in humanistic groups aims to free people from fears and anxieties by enabling a consciousness of their origin and a realistic appraisal of their meaning so that they can be dealt with in a practical way – little different in principle from the 'surfacing' process that we witnessed in psychotherapy (page 78). In the humanistic group, however, the context is not a medical one, the people have not been individually labelled as 'patients' and they probably regard themselves and are regarded by others as 'normal' and 'well'. Nevertheless, an interest in personal growth often leads to experience that may properly be described as therapeutic because the participant's feeling is one of increased freedom and well-being. If we are to consider health as something more than the mere absence of illness then the humanistic group is about the development of health. It attempts to promote growth in the individual's capacity to function safely and optionally in the face of varying environmental demands. This is not achieved in an objective or manipulative way where the goals are externally set; rather it is the result of the person, working in an atmosphere of acceptance and security, beginning both to value and evaluate himself, becoming responsible for his own actions and achieving a degree of autonomy in his life and his dealings with others.

The Mind-Body Unity

Yet another way of looking at health is from the viewpoint of prevention, especially in the reversal of destructive or dysfunctional tendencies. Many illnesses are due less to invasion by some hostile agent than to malfunction through excessive demand on an inadequate or an inadequately responding system. These are called pyschophysiological illnesses. People today are all too familiar with such conditions as ulceration of the stomach or intestinal tract, heart disease, headaches and skin disorders, and it is known that these and other so-called 'stress' diseases are due in part to the individual's *psychological* response to his work, family or other social environment in which he operates. Illness, therefore, may proceed through the perception of difficulty, the awareness of threat, the development of anxiety (ie. the psychological response) to the production of bodily symptoms of discomfort, irritation or pain and, perhaps, identifiable pathology (ie. the somatic response).

In recent decades the opposite view has been developed – that body posture, organisation and functioning affect the feelings – a view that is identified as the somato-psychic. Within this inverse process various techniques have emerged that aim to improve psychological comfort and well-being by working physically through the body; many of these use body contact of some kind to facilitate the release process.

Reich and his Followers
The contribution of Wilhelm Reich (1897–1957) lay in his observation that our psychological defences are reflected not only in established ways of thinking and acting and are predictable enough to be called personality characteristics, but also and significantly in the way we posture and control our bodies. This is to say that bodily expression corresponds to mental attitudes; in some people the *inhibition* of any strong emotion such as aggression, or even pleasure, is matched by dysfunctional changes in the musculature, increased or decreased muscle tone. Here Reich used an apt and much quoted metaphor; he referred to these new states of tension as the body's 'muscular armour'. It is a physical expression of personality 'armour' and its arrangement works to prevent our having a full and sensitive experience of the sensory

input available to us; it is so established as to create rigidity in thought and action, and a lack of spontaneity in these processes. Reich found that consistent work on the muscular defences using various kinds of massage resulted in a powerful and rapid release of the repressed energy accumulated from these withheld emotions.

Ida Rolf, whose own work was based on similar assumptions to those of Reich says: 'Materially speaking some muscles shorten and thicken ... others become immobilised by consolidation of the tissue involved. Once this has happened this physical attitude is invariable, it is involuntary; it can no longer be changed basically by taking thought or even by mental suggestion. Since it is not possible to establish a free tone through the physical flesh the subjective emotional tone becomes progressively more limited and tends to remain in a restricted, closely-defined area. Now what the individual feels is no longer an emotion, a response to an immediate situation, henceforth he lives, moves and has his being in an attitude'.

Most practitioners estimate that about ten one-or-two-hour sessions are needed to release and balance the muscles and to re-align the body posture. The manipulations involve more than the traditional massage, applying deep pressure on the normally soft tissue and employing the fingers, knuckles and even elbows to achieve this intense force. Rolf herself was nicknamed 'The Elbow' because this part of her body formed a powerful and sometimes painful tool in smoothing out muscular tension. One (perhaps unsympathetic) recipient of the Rolf technique reported that her desire to weep was due more to the searing pain of an elbow on her sternum than to any cathartic release. She did, however, also point out that one's attitude towards pain and the business of transcending it is an important part of the Rolfing experience (O'Sullivan 1979).

Downing (1979) assumes that the pain is due mainly to the release of what he calls 'tissue memories' held in the over-tense muscles – feelings that were too difficult to experience fully at the time of the original psychological or physical trauma.

He describes an example of such a release. Treating a patient for her fourth session, he began working on the inner leg muscles from the foot up to the inner attachments of the thigh along the inner bony surface of the pelvis. He relates how these muscles surrounding the sexual organs were abnormally tense so that as he manipulated and released each muscle in turn his patient gasped with pain. When asked why she thought this was the case she explained how the nuns who were once her schoolteachers were very strict, making all the girls keep their knees together on social occasions. All the way through school they were obliged to keep their legs crossed or closed so that it eventually became a habit.

Downing goes on to describe how the release of tension in these muscles led his client to achieve greater satisfaction from sexual intercourse.

Growth Activities

Not all of this bodywork in the tradition of Reich and his followers is directed at reposturing or catharsis. Schutz (1967) has described several games and exercises for understanding how we relate to other people, using a physical expression of, say, one's feelings of isolation, happiness, trust or aggression. Schutz argues that there are three areas of need in the development of a relationship: inclusion (ie. to belong to or be included by others), control (ie. to have influence and decision-making power), and affection. He gives examples of the physical contact established in order to work through people's difficulties in each of these areas. One was of a 'dowdy looking middle-aged plump school psychologist . . . named Henrietta! In a game called "New Names" she asked to be given a name which was the opposite of the way she appeared and felt – "Bubbles" '.

After some time this new name seemed to have made little difference and ' . . . she was still stiff and subdued enough for one member of the group to say that sometimes he felt like shaking her. Following the principle of converting feelings into actions he was asked if he would actually do it. He got up, took Bubbles by the shoulders and shook her up and down until they were bouncing all over the room with tremendous vigour. Bubbles began to effervesce. Her face was ruddy and she glowed. She was literally bubbly. A side of her that had never been shown began to emerge. She was cute, frisky, mischievous and she excelled at repartee. This pattern continued as she became more adventurous in the behaviour she was willing to try. At the end of the . . . (workshop) . . . she was exuberant and actually made attempts back at work, for the first few weeks, to have people call her "Bubbles" '.

Schutz described other physically-demanding activities in which individuals are given scope to come to terms with their feelings towards others. In one of these a woman has difficulty in making any contribution to the group and in explaining her feelings about this. 'When attention was focused on her it became clear that one of her central problems was trust. She didn't trust the group. To make this feeling sharper she was asked to fall backwards and rely on the leader – the one whom she distrusted least – to catch her. This was virtually impossible for her to do. After further exploration she was to try the roll and rock, to again experience her feelings about trust and also perhaps to go further into her difficulty. The following is Evelyn's description of her experience.

'*Evelyn's account*: "Then the group surrounded me in a tight circle and I was told to roll against them. With a feeling of relief I fell backwards into the bodies, some firm, some soft as I was propelled around the alternating men and women making up the amazingly secure enclosure which did not seem to yield in any way against my weight. Someone told me to relax my knees, so I collapsed them to find I was already totally supported by the members who easily and almost weightlessly passed me from one to another.

There was no sense of self – just of movement and strong hands supporting me as I was passed around and around. I felt blissful, as though it could go on forever." '

The account continues in a similar vein. It becomes clear from this that Evelyn learns to appreciate the basis for her own original mistrust of groups and begins to be able to express herself more freely through an increased trust in others.

Another interesting and comparable awareness activity based largely although not wholly on touching is the sensory awakening method of Bernard Gunther, one of the humanistic leaders at the growth centre at Esalen in California. In his unusual book *Sense Relaxation Below Your Mind* (1969) he stimulates and explains with words and photographs how we might set about re-educating our senses which, he says, are neither fully used nor properly integrated. He aims to increase our awareness in the 'here-and-now' and to broaden the way in which we conceive of and respond to the many familiar experiences of ourselves and our immediate surroundings. This is achieved by a variety of touching activities: tapping, slapping, shaking, lifting and stretching both one's own and another person's body; by a series of 'intimate games' such as touching between partners' backs, hands or heads, making 'conversations' with body parts and 'dancing' with the hands, the arms or shoulders; similar kinds of activity are prescribed for groups of people though some, like Evelyn's experience described above, can only be achieved with a group of about seven or more and have their own special quality for that reason.

In all of these activities the aim is to appreciate the very fundamentals of living and being; of breathing and feeling; of relaxing and becoming open to the stream of experience, and not to intellectualise or fantasise about what is happening. Thus, sensory awakening using these methods is a way to re-sensitise the body, or, as Gunther says, a way 'to become more conscious of the rich potentiality within us'.

In the same vein as Gunther, although more direct and

purposeful, is the prescription of Sidney Simon (1976) for touching to care for others. Simon speaks of 'skin hunger' as though we all need regular nourishment through contact with others. He says: 'Every human being comes into the world needing to be touched, and the need for skin contact persists until death, despite society's efforts to make us believe otherwise.'

He argues that this kind of touching is quite distinct from sexual contact and suggests, like Gunther, a number of exercises which can be used by pairs, trios and groups. Importantly, these exercises, called touch nourishment strategies, are outlined for the benefit of the family itself. Simon believes from his experience in teaching courses in these areas, that satisfaction of the touch hunger leads to body openness, better communications, less need for the abnormal stimulus of food and drugs and more gentle, loving relationships with others in the family.

Massage

Ordinary or Swedish massage is also used as a type of 'awareness contact'. Properly, the act of massaging another person's body is an act of helping and caring. A number of books on massage, some lavishly not to say erotically illustrated, have appeared recently, testifying to an increased interest in and demand for information about massage. This may be part of what one section of public opinion sees as a growing narcissistic trend in Western society whereas others regard such interest as an inevitable and largely adaptive response to the stresses and uncertainties of our ever-more-complex society – a sort of self-care activity, an identification with the most fundamental in human activity and experience. Thus George Downing, in *The Massage Book* (1972) says: ' . . . contrary to myth, massage is a healing art and not an advanced sexual technique'. This book carries detailed do-it-yourself instructions for beginning massage, for developing the techniques for giving and (the not entirely passive business of) receiving massage from another person.

As the receiver of massage one is encouraged to focus on one's own body, to be aware of its sensations, generally directing one's thoughts inwardly, perhaps on the breathing pattern or on the downward passage of breath towards the pelvis. As in much other 'growth activity' the person attends to the 'here-and-now', to the experience of the touch. This is not an intellectual appreciation, or an attempt to analyse the elements of or the intention behind the movement; rather it is an intuitive, direct response to the quality of the experience. George Downing compares it to listening to the '. . . sound of someone's voice without paying any attention to the meaning of the words'.

Massage of this kind is a continuous flow of non-verbal communication and to sense this best quality it is normally carried out in silence. Like the massage described in other sections of this book (Chapters 5 & 7), it has a therapeutic value, particularly in attempting to relieve excessively-tense areas. For example, the tension that is often apparent in a person's face may be eased by symmetrical movements from the centre line outwards mainly using gentle pressure of the thumbs. For a beginner, the massage technique is easy to learn and unique to experience since our faces are little touched by others, especially in a systematic way.

In Conclusion

We have looked at a few of the activities involving touch that are collectively under the title of humanistic experience. Some of these are plainly seen to bridge the gap between 'growth' activity and medicine or therapy. Indeed, the methods of Reich and Rolf have in some places been taken up by medical doctors. Whether these techniques are used by health professionals or by trained 'lay' practitioners, they require special skill in manipulation and the ability to assist the catharsis or emotional release that occurs simultaneously. For growth experience using the medium of touch (and many approaches to humanistic psychology in action do *not* require participants to touch each other), the methods of

Schultz and Gunther are gentler and easier to assimilate into one's continuing experience, but even here a leader with understanding of the growth process, a caring attitude and sensitivity to the individuals around him is needed to facilitate the personal learning with deftness and assurance.

What proof is there that these methods work? How do we know that they create beneficial changes? Of course, there is no unequivocal answer to either of these questions. The evidence is in the fact that humanistic psychology has grown rapidly both in this country and around the world, especially in the United States where it first began. Because the humanistic movement is concerned primarily with *people* and not minds or bodies or even mind-body processes, there can be no orthodox scientific explanation that fully accounts for what happens in the growth group.

We have seen in both massage and sensory awakening that personal attitudes are a vital part of the experience, if not the mainspring of the whole activity. Cynics and others who participate in a superficial way may not profit from what happens to them. Nevertheless, this kind of experience does not necessarily have the means of meeting everybody's needs. It is to be approached with an awareness of oneself and an openness to the effects. In one sense it is a paradox to be writing of its importance. The true value of the humanistic experience is in being in a group and having a full part in what takes place.

8 | Looking Ahead

Having examined what is being achieved through the use of touch in medicine, therapy and humanistic groups it is appropriate to consider the implications of these findings for the future of the caring process and for the education and preparation of health practitioners. Given that there is some weight to the evidence for the greater employment of touch as a generally positive agent in healing, there are still difficulties to be overcome.

In the clinical or nursing situation the kind of touching that occurs is largely controlled by the physical environment and the expectations of client and practitioner. Those who break these socially-defined boundaries must either plainly re-negotiate the conditions of the caring process or suffer discrediting or labelling as 'cranks' or 'quacks'. Indeed, current attitudes towards physical contact may be such that the act of touching is regarded as one of the 'problems' associated with the treatment of a client; that touching must be suppressed or channelled into the code of clinical objectivity for fear either of misrepresentation or personal involvement. Deviation from the accepted frame of reference is thought to imply unprofessional conduct.

Within this existing situation, however, we believe that there is scope for the development of closer and more frequent contact between the carer and the cared for. Previous chapters show that touching as an act of caring and healing implies physical, social and, indeed, personal skill. The practitioner is almost inevitably committed to the understanding and development of all three aspects of this activity.

In many professional courses the opportunity for fostering such skills is extremely limited. Our own experience is mainly with students of physiotherapy where body contact skills are more commonly used and it is within this context that the educational possibilities are illustrated, although what is described could, in principle, apply to the education of other health professionals also.

Development of Physical Skill

Physiotherapists spend relatively large amounts of their time in physical contact with the patient. Techniques designed to assess and treat disability demand a high degree of manual skill. One such skill, that of massage, is nowadays free from the obligations of formal examination and may therefore be more fully exploited as a rich medium for professional education in this sphere. It assists the achievement of greater sensitivity to and understanding of the client complementing the more academic and mechanistic approaches to his care. Its inclusion in physiotherapy courses (and we propose its consideration in courses for the preparation of other health care specialists) is justified on three counts:

1 it remains an ancient and valuable therapeutic modality in its own right, with recognised techniques and a number of documented effects (Chapter 5).
2 in the process of applying massage the student becomes familiar with the body structure and quality, and acquires manual skills which act as a base for more complex applications such as spinal and peripheral joint manipulations and neuro-developmental approaches to sufferers from stroke.
3 it represents a learning process in which, with some guidance as well as an element of personal discovery, one can establish a therapeutic relationship and an important channel of non-verbal communication.

In connection with these points, Maitland (1971) argues

that there is a need to develop new concepts in the way that manual skills are taught, so that students at postgraduate and undergraduate levels can gain a high level of sensitivity to both the signs and symptoms presented by the client. He reasons that a number of specialised techniques would be learnt more readily if students could bring to the classroom an ability to handle tissues in a tactually perceptive way. Such 'concepts' may be either perceptual-motor or verbal. Verbal concepts identify the tactile and kinaesthetic experience of the therapist, in the execution of manual skills, enabling these to be described to the student or to another practitioner. The acquisition of perceptual-motor concepts or schema, that is of the precise actions of and reactions to the hands in the acts of holding, palpating and moving the client's body, must be acquired mainly by doing. The practitioner, working through his hands, becomes more sensitive and more positive in his application. To illustrate this process we describe a session typifying the experience that is planned for students at the beginning of a course on massage.

Preliminary exercises   Students work in pairs, one acting as operator the other as model, using any part of the body (eg. the arm) which is to be free of clothing. The operator places her hands on the chosen part of the model's body. The hands then move in a flowing movement over this part following each contour; students attempt to identify not the anatomical entities but the different sensations discovered from areas of smoothness or hairiness; from protuberances and hollows, tender, ticklish or insensitive areas in their model. The important thing at this point is to concentrate on the feeling and sensation that is experienced.

The model tenses his arm and the operator identifies the differences now apparent.

The operator chooses an easily identifiable region such as the elbow or the knee. With her eyes closed she finds the boundaries and margins of any structure in that area.

Each operator does the same on several different models.

Each model attends to the sensation of being touched and prodded, analysing his response to this.

Discussion   Students are then encouraged to discuss their reactions to the task, on both sides of the practice, paying particular attention to the tactual quality of the experience and their own personal reaction to this.

Development of Social Skill in Touching

Argyle (1972) is a leading exponent of the idea that socially-effective behaviour is learned and practised in much the same way as a physical skill. He argues that our goal-directed interaction with another person seeks to achieve its ends by continuously adjusting to accommodate the changes in the other's behaviour.

Considering touch as a social skill, therefore, it is in the communication of certain social values such as understanding, competence, guidance and care, that the practitioner must be sensitive and proficient. He requires both an accurate picture of how the client is responding and, in view of this, the blend of actions which will equally accurately provide the care of which the client has need. This process implies that the practitioner knows or can get to know exactly what the client's needs are and even then they will be defined in the practitioner's own terms.

Seen in this way the appropriate and sensitive use of touch as an act of healing depends on the practitioner's own understanding not only of the client's anatomical and physiological responses, but also of all the other aspects of his behaviour. Thus, he must be able to understand the client's account of his symptoms, including his continuing responses during the exchange. He must pick up the many subtle but basic indications of feeling and attitude that are conveyed from the client by non-verbal means, as, for example in the voice quality and the variety of information expressed by the face and the eyes.

The touching behaviour that meets these expressed needs, whether they are for the reduction of muscular tension, the treatment of an injury or the care, love or simply the concern of another, will, ideally, take into account this wide range of information available and will provide this contact to the best possible effect.

The model of touching as social skill is, as we shall see, a limited one. However, it does have the merit of drawing our attention to the psychological mechanisms inherent in the situation; to the means by which the practitioner-client ends (ideally these would be common or shared ends) are to be achieved. To some extent, as in the case of a guiding or supporting arm, the ends and the means are the same: the guidance or support *is* the care. Even here, though, there is opportunity for further or more sophisticated communication in the *manner* in which the support is given; in the extent to which the helper finely gauges the firmness and lift to promote both security and yet confidence in his charge; to meet physical need with humanity. Such understanding is achieved partly by academic study and discussion – raising awareness of the issues involved in communication, for example – and partly by practical experiment, as in the massage practice described above, particularly (as far as social skill development is concerned) in the discussion following the practice itself.

The Personal Skill of Touching

Touching another human in order to help him is, in the final analysis, a *personal* act. Although constrained and directed by the social and physical skills of the actor, it derives its deeper meaning and force from the human values and attitudes brought to the helping situation; it is part of a belief in 'tender loving care'; it springs from the ability to empathise with another person, to understand how he thinks and feels, to be able to share his world. In this sense the healing touch cannot be applied simply in relation to the client's signs and symptoms: it is not merely another clinical tool. Much more than this, it is part of the whole pattern of the client/practitioner relationship; it is, in this context of care, an act whose implications spread, like the ripples from a stone thrown into a pond, far beyond the place and moment of contact. As we learned earlier, the touching of another brings both persons immediately into the 'here-and-now'. It may both ask and answer the questions 'Who am I?' and 'Who are you?' It is to do with personal history, personality and the development of the self.

All this implies that the caring process in general and the act of touching within this cannot be reduced to a set of rules, but is unique to each pair or group of individuals committed to it. In this relationship the carer has fully to appreciate the special experience of his client – and to relate this to his own needs and capabilities. Both of these insights – to others and to oneself – are what are meant by *personal* skill. It implies an ability to relate one's own resources (intellectual, physical, emotional, perhaps spiritual, and others) and personality to those of the client.

Training (perhaps a better word is education) for these awarenesses is not easy to plan or carry out because it involves the voluntary commitment of students to activities that potentially are challenging to the person, provoking conflict and discomfort in some. To become more aware of ourselves we must prepare to discover some things that are unpleasant as well as some that are likeable.

Nevertheless, attempts have been made to introduce such experience to courses of preparation for health professionals (eg. Van Altaan 1980). This has been undertaken in physiotherapy by one of the authors (Pratt & Seddon 1979) in the form of 'sensitivity training'. Nine hours, in three equal sessions, were allotted to taking the students through a number of 'games' and exercises, each designed to increase their sensitivity towards others and to help them become more aware of their own emotional reactions in interpersonal encounters. These activities have been used in other contexts and were not designed specifically for physiotherapists. One such exercise was 'blind milling' where, with the eyes closed, participants had to make contact in pairs using hands with hands or backs against backs to do so. They were then able to explore and discuss their own subjective reactions to the experience, for example their feelings of embarrassment or curiosity, their like and dislike of different kinds of contact. Another exercise enabled one person, acting as though he were blind, to be taken on a guided tour on which he negotiated a number of obstacles. In this exercise no speaking was allowed so that all communication had to take place using bodily contact. Again, students were encouraged to discuss their experiences and feelings about the sessions.

The authors' impressions were that such sessions were well received by the students and seemed to create a good climate for this kind of learning. The response to questionnaires completed after the training sessions indicated that about 30% of the group thought they had learned something about themselves while 70% said they were more aware of others than at the beginning of the work.

Conclusion

One problem in the education of practitioners is in the relatedness of the academic and the practical, the links between theory and action. How much does each contribute to the other in the promotion of successful care activity? How can a proper knowledge of medical and other health principles be made compatible with a flexible and discerning attitude to the client's immediate and ultimate needs and the preservation of his autonomy and efforts to care for himself?

The approach we have discussed here has the advantage of tackling the problem from both levels. We learn from both thought and action, neither one necessarily preceding the other. To care for and to heal using touch is a complicated process requiring understanding at a general and a personal level, good judgement, empathy and skill. It begins with an awareness of one's own resources and the needs of others.

We will end with a note of reservation about our own ability to come to terms with the subject of touch in care practice. The experience of touching and being touched is essentially a private one. Further, its meaning depends upon a number of extraneous as well as inter-personal factors in a given situation. Again, the effects of touch are influenced by cultures and systems of thinking. For these reasons it is impossible (and perhaps not desirable) to be fully objective or very conclusive about the use of touch in caring for others. In spite of our attempts to identify touching activity in various categories and purposive forms, it remains on each occurrence a unique event depending on fundamental and perhaps pre-conscious mechanisms of communication. The optimum touching response is still a matter of personal experience and individual judgement for the practitioner. Whilst arguing strongly for its further study and extended use one cannot be dogmatic or uniformly prescriptive about this. In the final analysis it is probably beyond explanation, representing something of the instinctive, the intuitive or the spiritual, perhaps part of what some people prefer to call the art (as opposed to the science) of healing.

9 | References

Argyle M. (1972) *The Psychology of Interpersonal Behaviour.* Harmondsworth: Pelican Books.

Asch S. E. (1956) Studies of independence and submission to group pressure. 1: a minority of one against a unanimous majority. *Psychol. Monogr.*, 70(416)

Barr J. S. & Taslitz N. (1970) The influence of back massage on autonomic functions. *Phys. Ther.*, **50**(12), 1679–1691

Beard G. & Wood E. C. (1964) *Massage: Principles and Techniques.* Philadelphia: W. B. Saunders

Beecher H. K. (1959) *Measurement of Objective Responses.* Oxford University Press

Bernstein M. (1976) *Nuns.* Glasgow: Collins

Bond M. R. (1971) The relation of pain to the E P I, The Cornell Medical Index and the Whiteley Index of Hypochondriasis. *Br. J. Psychiatry*, **119**, 671–678

Bower T. (1977) *The Perceptual World of the Child.* Glasgow: Fontana/Open Books

Bowlby J. (1951) *Maternal Care and Mental Health.* Geneva: W H O/London: HMSO

Burnside I. M. (1973) Touching is talking. *Am. J. Nurs.*, **73** (12), 2060–2063

Burton A. B. & Heller L. G. (1964) The touching of the body. *Psychoanal. Rev.*, **51**, 122–134

Comfort A. (1975) *The Joy of Sex.* London: Quartet Books

Cyriax J. (1971) *Textbook of Orthopaedic Medicine Vol 2: Treatment by Manipulation, Massage and Injection.* London: Bailliere Tindall

Downing G. (1972) *The Massage Book*. Harmondsworth: Penguin Handbooks

Downing J. (1979) Rolfing: massage with a message. *Forum*, **12**(3)

Drillien C. M. (1959) Physical and mental handicap in the prematurely born. *J. Obstet. Gynaec. Br. Comm.*, **66**, 721–728

Drinker C. K. & Yoffey J. M. (1941) *Lymphatics, Lymph and Lymphoid Tissue: Their Physiological and Clinical Significance.* Harvard University Press

Dummer T. G. (1978) Osteopathy. In Hulke M. (ed) *Encyclopaedia of Alternate Medicine and Self Help.* London: Rider & Co

Eagle J. (1976) *Alternative Medicine*. London: Futura Publications

Farley F. H. & Davis A. A. (1978) Masseuses, men and massage parlours: an exploratory descriptive study. *J. Sex Marital Ther.*, **4**(3), 219–225

Frank L. (1957) Tactile communication. *Genet. Psychol. Monogr.*, **56**, 211–255

Gibson J. J. (1966) *The Senses considered as Perceptual Systems.* London: Allen & Unwin

Goffman I. (1968) *Stigma: Notes on the Management of Spoiled Identity.* Harmondsworth: Penguin Books

Grad B. (1961) The influence of an unorthodox method of treatment on wound healing in mice. *J. Int. Parapsychol.*, **3**, 5–24

Grad B. (1964) A telekinetic effect on plant growth. Part 2: Experiments involving treatment with saline in stoppered bottles. *J. Int. Parapsychol.*, **6**, 473–498

Green H. (1964) *I Never Promised you a Rose Garden*. London: Gollancz

Gunther B. (1969) *Sense Relaxation Below Your Mind*. London: Macdonald

Harlow H. F. & Harlow M. K. (1966) Social deprivation in monkeys. *Sci. Am.*, **207**, 137–146

Haywood J. (1975) *Information – A Prescription against Pain.* R C N Study of Nursing Care. London: R C N

Held R. & Hein A. (1963) Movement-produced stimulation in the development of visually-guided behaviour. *J. Comp. Physiol. Psychol.*, **56**, 607–613

Henley N. M. (1973) The politics of touch. In Brown P. (ed) *Radical Psychology.* New York: Colophon Books

Heron W. (1961) Cognitive and physiological effects of perceptual isolation. In Soloman P. (ed) *Sensory Deprivation.* Cambridge, Mass.: Harvard University Press

Hilgard E. R., Atkinson R. C. & Atkinson R. L. (1971) *Introduction to Psychology.* New York: Harcourt Brace Jovanovich

Hoag J. M., Cole W. V. & Bradford S. G. (1969) *Osteopathic Medicine.* New York: McGraw-Hill

Hollender M. H. (1970) The need or wish to be held. *Arch. Gen. Psychiatry*, **22**, 445–453

Hollender M. H., Luborsky L. & Scaramella T. (1968) Body contact and sexual enticement. *Arch. Gen. Psychiatry*, **20**, 118–191

Huang L. T., Phares R. & Hollender M. H. (1976) The wish to be held: a transcultural study. *Arch. Gen. Psychiatry*, **33**, 41–43

Janis I. (1971) *Stress and Frustration.* New York: Harcourt Brace Jovanovich

Jourard S. M. (1966) An exploratory study of body accessibility. *Br. J. Soc. Clin. Psychol.*, **5**, 221–231

Jourard S. M. & Rubin J. E. (1968) Self-disclosure and touching: a study of two modes of interpersonal encounter and their inter-relation. *J. Humanist. Psychol.*, **8**, 39–48

Kee C. (1980) Misfit under-fives. *Contact (Journal of the Pre-School Playgroups Association)*, April, 21

Keele C. E. & Neil (eds) (1961) *Sampson Wright's Applied Physiology.* Oxford University Press

Krieger D. (1972) The relationship of touch, with intent to help or to heal, to subjects' *in vivo* haemoglobin values: a study in personalised interaction. In *Proc. Am. Nurs.*

Assoc. 9th Nurs. Res. Conf., San Antonio, Texas, *21–23 March* (*1973*)

Krieger D. (1972) The response of *in vivo* human haemoglobin to an active healing therapy by direct laying-on of hands. *Hum. Dimensions*, **1**, 12–15

Krieger D. (1975) Healing by the laying-on of hands as a facilitator of bio-energetic change: the response of *in vivo* human haemoglobin. *Int. J. Psychoenerg. Syst.*, **4**

Laing R. D. (1959) *The Divided Self.* London: Tavistock Publications

Laing R. D. (1970) *Knots.* Harmondsworth: Penguin Books

Laing R. D. (1975) *The Politics of Experience.* Harmondsworth: Penguin Books

Lawrence D. H. (1974) *The Collected Short Stories of D. H. Lawrence.* London: Heinemann

Lawson-Wood D. & Lawson-Wood J. (1978) *First Aid at your Fingertips.* Health Science Press

Leboyer F. (1976) *Loving Hands: The Traditional Indian Art of Baby Massage.* New York: Knopf

Lilley J. (1973) *Centre of the Cyclone.* London: Paladin

Lomranz J. & Shapira A. (1974) Communicative patterns of self-disclosure and touching behaviour. *J. Psychol.*, **88**, 223–227

McCorkle R. (1974) Effects of touch on seriously ill patients. *Nurs. Res.*, **23**(2), 125–132

Maitland G. D. (1970) *Peripheral Manipulation.* London: Butterworth

Mann F. (1972) *Acupuncture: The Ancient Chinese Art of Healing and How it Works Scientifically.* New York: Random House

Melzack R. (1977) *The Puzzle of Pain.* Harmondsworth: Penguin Books

Melzack R. & Wall P. D. (1962) On the nature of cutaneous sensory mechanisms. *Brain*, **85**, 331

Miller J. (1978) *The Body in Question.* London: Cape

Mintz E. E. (1969) Touch and the psychoanalytic tradition. *Psychoanal. Rev.*, **56**(3), 365–376

Montagna W. & Parakkal F. F. (1974) *The Structure and Function of the Skin*. New York: Academic Press

Montagu A. (1977) *Touching: The Human Significance of the Skin*. New York: Harper & Row

Morris D. (1978) *Manwatching; A Field Guide to Human Behaviour*. Triad Panther

O'Sullivan S. (1979) *I've been Rolfed*. Daily Mail, 27 Nov.

Pemberton R. (1950) Physiology of massage. In *A M A Handbook of Physical Medicine and Rehabilitation*. Philadelphia: Blakiston

Penfold W. & Rasmussen T. (1950) *The Cerebral Cortex of Man*. London: Macmillan

Piaget J. (1954) *The Construction of Reality in the Child*. New York: Basic Books

Pratt J. W. & Seddon V. (1979) Sensivity training with preclinical students. *Physiotherapy*, **65**(10), 310–311

Preston T. (1973) When words fail. *Am. J. Nurs.*, **73**(12), 2064–2066

Rogers C. R. (1961) *On Becoming a Person*. Boston, Ma.: Houghton Mifflin

Rowan J. (1976) *Ordinary Ecstasy*. London: Routledge & Kegan Paul

Schutz W. (1976) *Joy*. Harmondsworth: Penguin Books

Scott I. A. (19—) Osteopathy. In *Chiropractic and Osteopathy*. Friends of the Healing Trust, 5 Thorn Park, Plymouth, Devon

Seitz P. F. D. (1950) Psychocutaneous conditioning during the first two weeks of life. *Psychosomatic Medicine*, **12**, 187

Senden M. von (1932) *Space and Sight*. Trans. Heath P. (1960) London: Methuen

Shirley M. (1939) A behaviour syndrome characterising prematurely-born children. *Child Dev.*, **10**, 115–128

Simon S. B. (1976) *Caring, Feeling, Touching*. Argus Communications

Spotnitz H. (1972) Touch countertransference in group psychotherapy. *Int. J. Group Psychother.*, **22**(4), 455–463

St Luke the Apostle. The Gospel according to St Luke. In

The Holy Bible, Authorised Version, ch 12. v 13

Stoddard A. (1977) *Manual of Osteopathic Practice.* London: Hutchinson

Storey D. (1968) *This Sporting Life.* Harlow: Longmans

Straker M. (1962) Comparative studies of effects of normal and Caesarian delivery upon later manifestations of anxiety. *Compr. Psychiat.,* **3,** 113–124

Terkel S. (1977) The sporting life. In *Working.* Harmondsworth: Penguin Books

Van-Altaan M. (1980) A counselling course. *Health Visitor,* **53**(3), 93–96

Warwick R. & Williams P. L. (1973) *Gray's Anatomy.* Harlow: Longmans

Watson W. H. (1975) The meaning of touch: geriatric nursing. *J. Commun.,* **25**(3), 104–112

Index